THE BOOK
OF ACTS

NOTES COMPILED BY
DR. DAN C. HAMMER

Published at Sonrise Christian Center in Everett, WA.

ISBN: 9781793889928

Ordering information: Special discounts are available on quantity purchases.
For details, contact bookstore@isonrise.org

How To Use This Book

This is a compilation of sermon and study notes for the book of Acts. Dr. Hammer has used these notes throughout the years to preach and teach the various subjects covered in the Book of Acts. His orginal inspiration for the teaching of the book of Acts came from Dr. Don Camout's teaching from his time at Westgate Chapel, Edmonds Washington. Dr. Hammer hopes you will be able to utilize these notes for your own or those you lead into a deeper study and understanding of the Book of Acts.

Table of **Contents**

BOOK OF ACTS SERIES | LESSON 1

YOU SHALL RECEIVE POWER

Acts 1:1-11 - The former account I made, O Theophilus, of all that Jesus began both to do and teach, 2 until the day in which He was taken up, after He through the Holy Spirit had given commandments to the apostles whom He had chosen, 3 to whom He also presented Himself alive after His suffering by many infallible proofs, being seen by them during forty days and speaking of the things pertaining to the kingdom of God. 4 And being assembled together with them, He commanded them not to depart from Jerusalem, but to wait for the Promise of the Father, "which," He said, "you have heard from Me; 5 for John truly baptized with water, but you shall be baptized with the Holy Spirit not many days from now." 6 Therefore, when they had come together, they asked Him, saying, "Lord, will You at this time restore the kingdom to Israel?" 7 And He said to them, "It is not for you to know times or seasons which the Father has put in His own authority. 8 But you shall receive power when the Holy Spirit has come upon you; and you shall be witnesses to Me in Jerusalem, and in all Judea and Samaria, and to the end of the earth." 9 Now when He had spoken these things, while they watched, He was taken up, and a cloud received Him out of their sight. 10 And while they looked steadfastly toward heaven as He went up, behold, two men stood by them in white apparel, 11 who also said, "Men of Galilee, why do you stand gazing up into heaven? This same Jesus, who was taken up from you into heaven, will so come in like manner as you saw Him go into heaven."

INTRODUCTION:

A. The book of Acts is God's training manual. God wants us to be participants on the stage of history, not spectators. Live it!

B. This book was written by Doctor Luke.

   1. Colossians 4:14 - *Luke the beloved physician....*

   2. Philemon 24 - *. . . . as do Mark, Aristarchus, Demas, Luke, my fellow laborers.*

   3. 2 Timothy 4:11 - *Only Luke is with me. Get Mark and bring him with you, for he is useful to me for ministry.*

   4. He had great literary skills.

   5. He used technical physician terms.

   6. 'The Gospel of Luke tells us what Jesus did; the Book of Acts tells what He expected His followers to do.' - F.F. Bruce

   7. Let's look at how we can learn and teach all that Jesus taught us and help finish what He began.

I. Pertaining To The Kingdom Of God. (V1-3)

A. Luke recorded the accounts of Jesus' actions and teachings.

   1. Acts recounts where Jesus began.

   2. To Theophilus he wrote an accurate and historical report.

      a. Actions and teaching go together.

      b. The way you act affects the way you teach.

   3. It covered what Jesus did between His resurrection and His ascension.

      a. He was taken up.

      b. After His ascension, through the Holy Spirit, Jesus gave commandments to His chosen apostles.

         i. Acts 10:38 - *...how God anointed Jesus of Nazareth with the Holy Spirit and with power, who went about doing good and healing all who were oppressed by the devil, for God was with Him.*

         ii. The power of the Holy Spirit that operated through Jesus, through the apostles, and through the early church can operate through you!

B. He spoke of things pertaining to the kingdom of God.

   1. Jesus presented himself alive for forty days after his sufferings. There are many infallible proofs.

2. He poured out the details of the kingdom of God.
    a. What is the kingdom of God?
        i.   It is present where Jesus is acknowledged as Lord and King.
        ii. A spiritual kingdom that has visible manifestations on the earth.
        iii. It is present and future.
        iv. Jesus will present or deliver the kingdom to His Father. When the last enemy is destroyed.
             - Death (I Corinthians 15:24-26) And there will be a new heaven and a new earth
             (Revelation 21:1)
        v.   John the Baptist declared, 'The kingdom of heaven is at hand.' (Matthew 3:2,) Jesus came
             preaching the gospel of the kingdom. (Matthew 4:23) And the disciples preached, 'The
             kingdom of heaven is at hand.' (Matthew 10:7)
        vi. Jesus declared war on the kingdom of darkness.
            a.) I John 3:8 - *He who sins is of the devil, for the devil has sinned from the beginning For this
                purpose the Son of God was manifested, that He might destroy the works of the devil.*
            b.) Matthew 11:11-12 - *...now the kingdom of heaven suffers violence, and the violent take it
                by force.* He recruited, empowered and released people.
        vii. Matthew 6:10 - *Your kingdom come. Your will be done on earth as it is in heaven.*
        viii. In Isaiah 61, the Gospel preached to the poor, Brokenhearted healed Captives delivered,
             Sight for the blind, Oppressed liberated Acceptable year of the Lord preached
    b. The keys of the kingdom - binding and loosing. (Matthew 16: 18-19)

APPLICATION
    A. The kingdom of heaven is at hand!
    B. The kingdom of God is advancing and warring against the kingdom of darkness.
    C. Matthew 6:33 - *But seek first the kingdom of God and His righteousness, and all these things shall be
       added to you.*
    D. We are a Spirit-filled church family bringing the kingdom of heaven to earth.

II. **Pertaining To The Promises Of The Father....You Shall Receive Power.**
    A. He told them to go then then He said 'wait'.
        1. He commanded them not to depart from Jerusalem.
        2. They were to wait for the promise of the Father.
            a. Luke 24:49 - *Behold, I send the Promise of My Father upon you; but tarry in the city of
               Jerusalem until you are endued with power from on high.*
            b. The promise of the Baptism of the Holy Spirit! They waited a good portion of the 10 days in
               the Upper Room. Wait on God! Wait on His promises!
            c. John baptized with water, but you shall be baptized with the Holy Spirit.
    B. They asked, "When will you restore the kingdom to Israel?"
        1. They had not understood the kingdom of God.
        2. "At this time will you restore?", showed they meant a political and territorial kingdom was what
           they were looking for.
    C. He told them it was not for them to know times or seasons. This will be the Father's business.
    D. But you shall receive power after the Holy Spirit has come upon you.
        1. Resulting in being witnesses and martyrs.
        2. In Jerusalem, Judea, Samaria and to the ends of the earth.
        3. Power to witness!
    E. Jesus ascended according to the Father's promise.
        1. He was taken up and received in a cloud out of their sight.
        2. Two men in white appeared and said, 'Men of Galilee why are you gazing into heaven?'

APPLICATION

    A. You shall receive power!

    B. Power to be witnesses!

    C. Power to advance the kingdom.

    D. Power to do and teach.

BOOK OF ACTS SERIES | LESSON 2
MEN AND WOMEN OF PRAYER

Acts 1:12-26 - *Then they returned to Jerusalem from the mount called Olivet, which is near Jerusalem, a Sabbath day's journey. 13 And when they had entered, they went up into the upper room where they were staying: Peter, James, John, and Andrew; Philip and Thomas; Bartholomew and Matthew; James the son of Alphaeus and Simon the Zealot; and Judas the son of James. 14 These all continued with one accord in prayer and supplication, with the women and Mary the mother of Jesus, and with His brothers. 15 And in those days Peter stood up in the midst of the disciples (altogether the number of names was about a hundred and twenty), and said, 16 "Men and brethren, this Scripture had to be fulfilled, which the Holy Spirit spoke before by the mouth of David concerning Judas, who became a guide to those who arrested Jesus; 17 for he was numbered with us and obtained a part in this ministry." 18 (Now this man purchased a field with the wages of iniquity; and falling headlong, he burst open in the middle and all his [e]entrails gushed out. 19 And it became known to all those dwelling in Jerusalem; so that field is called in their own language, Akel Dama, that is, Field of Blood.) 20 "For it is written in the Book of Psalms: 'Let his dwelling place be desolate, And let no one live in it'; and, 'Let another take his office.' 21 "Therefore, of these men who have accompanied us all the time that the Lord Jesus went in and out among us, 22 beginning from the baptism of John to that day when He was taken up from us, one of these must become a witness with us of His resurrection." 23 And they proposed two: Joseph called Barsabas, who was surnamed Justus, and Matthias. 24 And they prayed and said, "You, O Lord, who know the hearts of all, show which of these two You have chosen 25 to take part in this ministry and apostleship from which Judas by transgression fell, that he might go to his own place." 26 And they cast their lots, and the lot fell on Matthias. And he was numbered with the eleven apostles.*

INTRODUCTION
A. Luke 24:53 - *and were continually in the temple praising and blessing God. Amen.*
B. Luke 24:49 - *Behold, I send the Promise of My Father upon you; but tarry in the city of Jerusalem until you are endued with power from on high.*
C. The men and women who had been with Jesus were in a ten day prayer meeting waiting for the promise of the Father. They had returned Jerusalem from the Mount of Olives, a Sabbath day's journey. Approximately 1/2 to 3/4 of a mile away.
D. God still uses and gathers men around Him who wait on Him and are intimate with Him. Let's look at Acts 1:2-26.

I. Who Are The Men And Women Of Prayer?
A. In the Upper Room.
   1. Men in the Upper Room: Peter, James, John, Andrew, Philip, Thomas, Bartholomew, Matthew, James the son of Alphaeus, Simon the Zealot and Judas the son of James and Jesus' brothers.
   2. Women in the Upper Room
      a. With the women, Mary the mother of Jesus.
      b. Luke 8:2-3 - *. . . .and certain women who had been healed of evil spirits and infirmities - Mary called Magdalene, out of whom had come seven demons, and Joanna the wife of Chuza, Herod's steward, and Susanna, and many others who provided for Him from their substance.*
B. They all continued in one accord in prayer and supplication.
   1. Colossians 4:2 - *Continue earnestly in prayer, being vigilant in it with thanksgiving;"*
   2. I Thessalonians 5:17 - *. . . .pray without ceasing. . . .*
   3. James 5:16 - *The effective, fervent prayer of a righteous man avails much.*
   4. Psalm 133 - *Brethren in unity. We need to be in accord.*

APPLICATION
A. Great men and great women pray.
B. Great men and great women continue in prayer.
C. Great men and great women are in one accord in prayer.

II. Men And Women In Prayer - Put People In Place.
A. Replacing Judas
1. Peter stood up and said what Psalms said concerning Judas.
a. Psalm 69:25 - *Let their dwelling place be desolate; let no one live in their tents.*
b. Psalm 109:8 - *Let his days be few, and let another take his office.*
c. Sad, but some will perish. Hell is real.
d. Judas committed suicide.
e. 'Let another take his office.'
2. They chose two.
a. They had to have been with Jesus from the time that John baptized Him.
b. They were witnesses of His ministry, death and resurrection.
c. Joseph and Matthias
d. They cast lots and Matthias was chosen.
e. Matthias was numbered with the eleven apostles.

APPLICATION
A. Praying people birth others with their prayers.
B. I Corinthians 12:18 - *But now God has set the members, each of them, in the body just as He pleased.*
C. Joseph or Matthias - God knows.
D. Where is your place? Prayer places people.

PENTECOST

Acts 2:1-39 - *When the Day of Pentecost had fully come, they were all with one accord in one place. 2 And suddenly there came a sound from heaven, as of a rushing mighty wind, and it filled the whole house where they were sitting. 3 Then there appeared to them divided tongues, as of fire, and one sat upon each of them. 4 And they were all filled with the Holy Spirit and began to speak with other tongues, as the Spirit gave them utterance. 5 And there were dwelling in Jerusalem Jews, devout men, from every nation under heaven. 6 And when this sound occurred, the multitude came together, and were confused, because everyone heard them speak in his own language. 7 Then they were all amazed and marveled, saying to one another, "Look, are not all these who speak Galileans? 8 And how is it that we hear, each in our own language in which we were born? 9 Parthians and Medes and Elamites, those dwelling in Mesopotamia, Judea and Cappadocia, Pontus and Asia, 10 Phrygia and Pamphylia, Egypt and the parts of Libya adjoining Cyrene, visitors from Rome, both Jews and proselytes, 11 Cretans and Arabs—we hear them speaking in our own tongues the wonderful works of God." 12 So they were all amazed and perplexed, saying to one another, "Whatever could this mean?" 13 Others mocking said, "They are full of new wine." 14 But Peter, standing up with the eleven, raised his voice and said to them, "Men of Judea and all who dwell in Jerusalem, let this be known to you, and heed my words. 15 For these are not drunk, as you suppose, since it is only the third hour of the day. 16 But this is what was spoken by the prophet Joel: 17 'And it shall come to pass in the last days, says God, That I will pour out of My Spirit on all flesh; Your sons and your daughters shall prophesy, Your young men shall see visions, Your old men shall dream dreams. 18 And on My menservants and on My maidservants I will pour out My Spirit in those days; And they shall prophesy. 19 I will show wonders in heaven above And signs in the earth beneath: Blood and fire and vapor of smoke. 20 The sun shall be turned into darkness, And the moon into blood, Before the coming of the great and awesome day of the Lord. 21 And it shall come to pass That whoever calls on the name of the Lord Shall be saved.' 22 "Men of Israel, hear these words: Jesus of Nazareth, a Man attested by God to you by miracles, wonders, and signs which God did through Him in your midst, as you yourselves also know— 23 Him, being delivered by the determined purpose and foreknowledge of God, you have taken by lawless hands, have crucified, and put to death; 24 whom God raised up, having loosed the pains of death, because it was not possible that He should be held by it. 25 For David says concerning Him: 'I foresaw the Lord always before my face, For He is at my right hand, that I may not be shaken. 26 Therefore my heart rejoiced, and my tongue was glad; Moreover my flesh also will rest in hope. 27 For You will not leave my soul in Hades, Nor will You allow Your Holy One to see corruption. 28 You have made known to me the ways of life; You will make me full of joy in Your presence.' 29 "Men and brethren, let me speak freely to you of the patriarch David, that he is both dead and buried, and his tomb is with us to this day. 30 Therefore, being a prophet, and knowing that God had sworn with an oath to him that of the fruit of his body, according to the flesh, He would raise up the Christ to sit on his throne, 31 he, foreseeing this, spoke concerning the resurrection of the Christ, that His soul was not left in Hades, nor did His flesh see corruption. 32 This Jesus God has raised up, of which we are all witnesses. 33 Therefore being exalted to the right hand of God, and having received from the Father the promise of the Holy Spirit, He poured out this which you now see and hear. 34 "For David did not ascend into the heavens, but he says himself: 'The Lord said to my Lord, "Sit at My right hand, 35 Till I make Your enemies Your footstool." ' 36 "Therefore let all the house of Israel know assuredly that God has made this Jesus, whom you crucified, both Lord and Christ." 37 Now when they heard this, they were cut to the heart, and said to Peter and the rest of the apostles, "Men and brethren, what shall we do?" 38 Then Peter said to them, "Repent, and let every one of you be baptized in the name of Jesus Christ for the remission of sins; and you shall receive the gift of the Holy Spirit. 39 For the promise is to you and to your children, and to all who are afar off, as many as the Lord our God will call."*

INTRODUCTION

A. Day of Pentecost means 'fifty'. The annual Jewish festival scheduled for fifty days after Passover. It was called the 'Feast of Weeks' but also the 'Feast of Harvest' because the Jewish people presented the first fruits of the harvest.

B. The Pentecostal Movement.

C. This is the story of the formation of the church. These are our roots!

I. The Power Of Pentecost (V1-13)

A. The Day of Pentecost had fully come.
1. God has a 'full' time.
2. Ecclesiastes 3:1 - *To everything there is a season, a time for every purpose under heaven:*

B. They were experiencing the power of being in one accord.
1. With one accord = homothumadom (gr.) - being unanimous, having mutual consent, being in agreement, having group unity, having one mind and purpose.
2. In one place - waiting for the promise of the Father.

C. Suddenly the power came....
1. A sound from heaven...as of a rushing, mighty wind.
   a. John 3 - *The wind blows where it wishes, and you hear the sound of it, but cannot tell where it comes from and where it goes.*
   b. Ezekiel 37 - *Come from the four winds....*
   c. It filled the whole house.
2. There appeared to be tongues of fire sitting upon each oneof them.
   a. Fire represents the Spirit.
   b. The fire of the Holy Spirit burns out the dross, refines and galvanizes us.
   c. They were completely filled; made full.
   d. They began to speak in tongues as the Spirit gave them utterance.

D. This power caused the people to gather....
1. Devout people at Jerusalem - Jews from every nation under heaven.
2. They all heard them speak in tongues the wonderful works of God.
3. Galileans spoke Aramaic, but now by the Holy Spirit they spoke Latin, Greek and other languages. Luke records fifteen language groups.
4. They heard them speak about the wonderful works of God.
   a. Wonderful works-megaleios = conspicuous, magnificent, splendid, majestic, good, excellent, etc...
   b. They were amazed, perplexed and questioned each other, 'Whatever could this mean?' Others were mocking them saying, 'They are full of new wine.'

APPLICATION

A. God has a time.

B. God has a people. (expectant)

C. God has power!

II. The Preaching Of Pentecost (V14-39)

A. Preaching from the word of God.
1. They were not drunk at 9 am.
2. This is what Joel declared when he spoke about the outpouring of the Spirit on all flesh.
   a. Dreams
   b. Visions
   c. Prophecy
   d. Signs and wonders

3. This fulfilled Old Testament prophecy. The day of the Lord will come. He will come as a thief in the night.
B. Preaching centered on Jesus.
   1. Whosoever shall call on the name of the Lord shall be saved!
      a. Kerygma - a herald's announcement of the plain facts of the Christian message.
      b. Did ache - teaching the meaning of the facts.
      c. Paraklesis - exhortation to the living
      d. Homilia - discourse of subject matter pertaining to any area of Christian life.
   2. The person of Jesus Christ - Jesus of Nazareth, a man approved of God
   3. The works of Jesus Christ - Miracles, signs and wonders
   4. The Passion of Christ - Him being delivered by the defense of counsel and fore knowledge of God. It was God's will-divine side; wicked hands-man's side.
   5. The resurrection of Jesus Christ - God loosed us from the pain of death.
   6. The exaltation of Jesus Christ - He is at the right hand of the Father
   7. The outpouring of the Holy Spirit - Christ raised, the Spirit poured out
C. Preaching that brings a response.
   1. They heard this and were pricked in their hearts. They asked, 'What shall we do?'
   2. Peter replied:
      a. Repent.
      b. Be baptized every one of you.
      c. You shall receive the gift of the Holy Spirit - the presence is for all of you.
      d. Save yourselves from this perverse generation.

APPLICATION
   1. How do you respond to preaching?
   2. God loves you!
   3. This message is for you - RESPOND!

CONTINUING WHAT THE EARLY CHURCH STARTED

Acts 2:37-47 - Now when they heard this, they were cut to the heart, and said to Peter and the rest of the apostles, "Men and brethren, what shall we do?" 38 Then Peter said to them, "Repent, and let every one of you be baptized in the name of Jesus Christ for the remission of sins; and you shall receive the gift of the Holy Spirit. 39 For the promise is to you and to your children, and to all who are afar off, as many as the Lord our God will call." 40 And with many other words he testified and exhorted them, saying, "Be saved from this perverse generation." 41 Then those who gladly received his word were baptized; and that day about three thousand souls were added to them. 42 And they continued steadfastly in the apostles' doctrine and fellowship, in the breaking of bread, and in prayers. 43 Then fear came upon every soul, and many wonders and signs were done through the apostles. 44 Now all who believed were together, and had all things in common, 45 and sold their possessions and goods, and divided them among all, as anyone had need. 46 So continuing daily with one accord in the temple, and breaking bread from house to house, they ate their food with gladness and simplicity of heart, 47 praising God and having favor with all the people. And the Lord added to the church daily those who were being saved.

INTRODUCTION

A. John 8: 31-32 - *Then Jesus said to those Jews who believed Him, 'If you abide in My word, you are My disciples indeed. And you shall know the truth, and the truth shall make you free.'*
   1. Ghinocekoe - to perceive, understand, to recognize the truth by personal experience.
   2. There is freedom that comes from experiencing the truth.
B. The Day of Pentecost released the power of the Holy Spirit.
C. Let's see what the early church did so we can continue to do what they started.

I. The Early Church Was Evangelistic.

A. It brought a call.
   1. They were baptized in the Holy Spirit to preach the Gospel of the Kingdom.
   2. The Book of Corinthians says, "It is through the foolishness of preaching that men are saved."
B. It brought conviction.
   1. They were pricked in their hearts.
   2. Romans 3:23 - . . . .*for all have sinned and fall short of the glory of God.*
C. It brought conversion.
   1. They repented.
   2. 3,000 were saved.
D. It brought commitment.
   1. They were baptized in water. What a baptism service!
   2. They were baptized in the Holy Spirit.
   3. They were becoming members of the church.

APPLICATION: Let's continue evangelizing!

II. The Early Church Was A Teaching Church.

A. They taught the apostle's doctrine.
   1. didaskalos (gr.) - doctrine, learning, teaching; means to learn and to teach.
   2. They taught the word of God. 2 Timothy 3:16-17 - *All Scripture is given by inspiration of God, and is profitable for doctrine, for reproof, for correction, for instruction in righteousness, that the man of God may be complete, thoroughly equipped for every good work.*
   3. Read 2 Timothy 2:2

4. They probably taught what Jesus taught them for 40 days. (Acts 1:3)
B. They continued steadfastly.
 1. proskartereo (gr.) - to be earnest towards, i.e. to persevere, be constant, diligent, to adhere closely.
 2. 2 Timothy 2:15 - *Be diligent to present yourself approved to God, a worker who does not need to be ashamed, rightly dividing the word of truth.*

APPLICATION
 A. Let's continue steadfastly in the apostle's doctrine.
 B. Teach others. We not only teach others to "do" we train them to train up others.

III. The Early Church Was A Koinonia Church.
 A. They had fellowship.
  1. Koinonia - joint participation, partnership, social intercourse, communion.
  2. They bore and shared each others burdens.
  3. They met needs
 B. They had communion.
  1. The breaking of bread - communion and a meal. (v42)
  2. They prayed together. (v46, sharing needs)

APPLICATION: How am I fellowshipping? Let's share with one another!

IV. The Early Church Moved In Signs And Wonders.
 A. The fear of the Lord was upon all of them.
 B. They worked with God.
  1. He works with us.
  2. John 5:19,20
 C. They saw signs and wonders.
  1. Mark 16:17 - *And these signs will follow those who believe: In My name theywill cast out demons; they will speak with new tongues;*
  2. Mark 16:20 - *And they went out and preached everywhere, the Lord working with them and confirming the word through the accompanying signs. Amen.*

APPLICATION: God reveals himself. The apostolic church moved in power!

V. The Early Church Was A Sharing Community.
 A. They were caring.
  1. Love someone.
  2. Care by taking time for someone.
 B. They were in fellowship.
  1. They had a quality of togetherness.
  2. A church of brothers and sisters.
  3. Relationship - gladness
   a. They were together with a simplicity of heart.
   b. In one accord

APPLICATION
 A. Love
 B. Care
 C. Meet needs

VI. The Early Church Was A Church Of Praise And Worship.

A. They praised
   1. They praised God.
   2. Psalm 22:3 - *But You are holy, enthroned in the praises of Israel.*
   3. Praise is a release of faith.
B. Worship
   1. God is seeking worshippers. John 4:23-24
   2. Romans 12:1-2 is worship

APPLICATION: God gave them favor. They were attractive because they had been in the Lord's presence. Praise and worship.

THE NAME OF JESUS CHRIST OF NAZARETH

Acts 3 - Now Peter and John went up together to the temple at the hour of prayer, the ninth hour. 2 And a certain man lame from his mother's womb was carried, whom they laid daily at the gate of the temple which is called Beautiful, to ask alms from those who entered the temple; 3 who, seeing Peter and John about to go into the temple, asked for alms. 4 And fixing his eyes on him, with John, Peter said, "Look at us." 5 So he gave them his attention, expecting to receive something from them. 6 Then Peter said, "Silver and gold I do not have, but what I do have I give you: In the name of Jesus Christ of Nazareth, rise up and walk." 7 And he took him by the right hand and lifted him up, and immediately his feet and ankle bones received strength. 8 So he, leaping up, stood and walked and entered the temple with them—walking, leaping, and praising God. 9 And all the people saw him walking and praising God. 10 Then they knew that it was he who sat begging alms at the Beautiful Gate of the temple; and they were filled with wonder and amazement at what had happened to him. 11 Now as the lame man who was healed held on to Peter and John, all the people ran together to them in the porch which is called Solomon's, greatly amazed. 12 So when Peter saw it, he responded to the people: "Men of Israel, why do you marvel at this? Or why look so intently at us, as though by our own power or godliness we had made this man walk? 13 The God of Abraham, Isaac, and Jacob, the God of our fathers, glorified His Servant Jesus, whom you delivered up and denied in the presence of Pilate, when he was determined to let Him go. 14 But you denied the Holy One and the Just, and asked for a murderer to be granted to you, 15 and killed the Prince of life, whom God raised from the dead, of which we are witnesses. 16 And His name, through faith in His name, has made this man strong, whom you see and know. Yes, the faith which comes through Him has given him this perfect soundness in the presence of you all. 17 "Yet now, brethren, I know that you did it in ignorance, as did also your rulers. 18 But those things which God foretold by the mouth of all His prophets, that the Christ would suffer, He has thus fulfilled. 19 Repent therefore and be converted, that your sins may be blotted out, so that times of refreshing may come from the presence of the Lord, 20 and that He may send Jesus Christ, who was preached to you before, 21 whom heaven must receive until the times of restoration of all things, which God has spoken by the mouth of all His holy prophets since the world began. 22 For Moses truly said to the fathers, 'The Lord your God will raise up for you a Prophet like me from your brethren. Him you shall hear in all things, whatever He says to you. 23 And it shall be that every soul who will not hear that Prophet shall be utterly destroyed from among the people.' 24 Yes, and all the prophets, from Samuel and those who follow, as many as have spoken, have also foretold these days. 25 You are sons of the prophets, and of the covenant which God made with our fathers, saying to Abraham, 'And in your seed all the families of the earth shall be blessed.' 26 To you first, God, having raised up His Servant Jesus, sent Him to bless you, in turning away every one of you from your iniquities."

INTRODUCTION

   A. Names are significant.

   B. 'We readily admit that Jesus and all the genuine saints throughout history had spiritual power and that they had a deep prayer life. We believe that there must be some connection between their power and their life of prayer.'

   C. There is power and refreshing in the name of Jesus Christ of Nazareth. Let's look at the name of Jesus of Nazareth this morning and how it applies to us.

I. There Is Power In The Name Of Jesus Of Nazareth.

   A. Prayer is a key to this power.

      1. Peter and John went up together into the temple at the hour of prayer which was three in the afternoon. Prayer had gone on since Jesus arose!

2. James 5:16 - *The effective, fervent prayer of a righteous man avails much.*
B. Human need is a key to this power.
   1. He was a certain man known by God. God knows you. He was lame from his mother's womb and someone laid him at the Beautiful Gate daily.
   2. The Beautiful Gate was one of the gates of Herod's temple. It was probably on the east side of the temple. People are waiting outside the gate. A good place for a beggar to beg.
   3. The lame man asked Peter and John for alms. They fastened their eyes on him and said, 'Look at us.' They saw his need. He expected to receive one thing from them, but got something else.
C. His name is a key to power.
   1. 'Silver and gold I do not have, but what I do have I give to you. In the name of Jesus Christ of Nazareth, rise up and walk.' God was not only worked in them, but continued His work through them.
   2. John 14:13-14 - *And whatever you ask in My name, that I will do, that the Father may be glorified in the Son. If you ask anything in My name, I will do it.*
   3. Philippians 2:9-11 - *Therefore God also has highly exalted Him and given Him the name which is above every name, that at the name of Jesus every knee should bow, of those in heaven, and of those on earth, and of those under the earth, and that every tongue should confess that Jesus Christ is Lord, to the glory of God the Father.*
   4. Acts 16:18 - . . . .*But Paul, greatly annoyed, turned and said to the spirit, 'I command you in the name of Jesus Christ to come out of her.'* She was made whole.
   5. Why do we pray in the name of Jesus Christ of Nazareth?
      a. We pray in the name of Jesus Christ to acknowledge we have no right or access to come to the Father apart from Him!
      b. II Corinthians 1:20 - *For all the promises of God in Him are Yes, and in Him Amen, to the glory of God through us.*
      c. There is power in the name of Jesus Christ of Nazareth.
   6. What does the name of Jesus Christ entail?
      a. It is the transliteration of the Hebrew word, 'Joshua' meaning 'Jehovah is salvation.' His name reveals His character, His nature and His work.
      b. John 17:6 - *I have manifested Your name. . . .*
      c. To pray in the name of Jesus Christ of Nazareth is the Christian's power of attorney. The power of attorney means the legal and written authority to transact business for another.
   7. How do we pray in the name of Jesus of Nazareth?
      a. It should be an attitude of heart. It is not just a nice ending to a prayer. It is with a deep awareness of the worthiness of His name!
      b. We should pray believing He will do what He said He would.
      c. He took him by the right hand and said, 'Rise up and walk.' Strength entered his legs and he was walking, leaping and praising God. Luke used a medical term. 'Leaped up' means an unlocked socket, coming into place that which was out of place.
      d. We can bring His healing to a sinful and crippled world.
D. Humility is a key to power.
   1. The people ran to Solomon's porch and were astonished.
   2. Peter said don't marvel or look at us like our own power or holiness made this man walk.
      a. James 4:10 - *Humble yourselves in the sight of the Lord, and He will lift you up.*
      b. Give the glory to God.
   3. He pointed them to:
      a. The God of Abraham, Isaac and Jacob. The source.
      b. His Son, Jesus delivered up and denied in front of Pilate.
      c. His servant.
      d. The Holy One.
      e. The Just. (they asked for a murderer)

        f.   The Prince of Life. (the author and pioneer)

        g.   The Resurrection.

    4.   They killed Him, but they did it ignorantly.

    5.   Acts 3:16 - *And His name, through faith in His name, has made this man strong, whom you see and know. Yes, the faith which comes through Him has given him this perfect soundness in the presence of you all.*

APPLICATION

    A. Have faith in the name of Jesus Christ of Nazareth.   .

    B. The gifts of the Spirit are available and active (faith, healing, the working of miracles)

    C. Keys: prayer, human need, His name, humility

II. REFRESHING IN THE NAME OF JESUS CHRIST OF NAZARETH.

    A. The Key of Repentance.

        1.   'Repent therefore and be converted, that our sins may be blotted out.'

            a.   Repent - turn against or turn to

            b.   Turning from our former way of life to a new life of faith and obedience to Christ.

            c.   God gives us repentance, but we must receive it.

        2.   The goodness of God leads us to repent. Romans 2:4

    B. The Key of Refreshing.

        1.   The times of refreshing will come from the Lord, in His presence.

        2.   Hosea 10:12 - *Sow for yourselves righteousness; reap in mercy; break up your fallow ground, for it is time to seek the Lord, till He comes and rains righteousness on you.*

        3.   Matthew 11:28-30 - *Come to Me, all you who labor and are heavy laden, and I will give you rest. Take My yoke upon you and learn from Me, for I am gentle and lowly in heart, and you will find rest for your souls. For My yoke is easy and My burden is light.*

    C. The Key of Restoration.

        1.   Christ will come. He will return.

        2.   He will restore Israel. He will restore all that was spoken by the mouth of His holy prophets.

        3.   Moses-Samuel-Abraham-all the prophets pointed to Jesus.

        4.   He was sent to bless you! To turn us from iniquity! 'He will restore you.' Return to the original use.

APPLICATION

    A. There is power in the name of Jesus Christ of Nazareth for repentance.

    B. Refreshing

    C. Restoration

OPPOSITION

Acts 4 - *Now as they spoke to the people, the priests, the captain of the temple, and the Sadducees came upon them, 2 being greatly disturbed that they taught the people and preached in Jesus the resurrection from the dead. 3 And they laid hands on them, and put them in custody until the next day, for it was already evening. 4 However, many of those who heard the word believed; and the number of the men came to be about five thousand. 5 And it came to pass, on the next day, that their rulers, elders, and scribes, 6 as well as Annas the high priest, Caiaphas, John, and Alexander, and as many as were of the family of the high priest, were gathered together at Jerusalem. 7 And when they had set them in the midst, they asked, "By what power or by what name have you done this?" 8 Then Peter, filled with the Holy Spirit, said to them, "Rulers of the people and elders of Israel: 9 If we this day are judged for a good deed done to a helpless man, by what means he has been made well, 10 let it be known to you all, and to all the people of Israel, that by the name of Jesus Christ of Nazareth, whom you crucified, whom God raised from the dead, by Him this man stands here before you whole. 11 This is the 'stone which was rejected by you builders, which has become the chief cornerstone.' 12 Nor is there salvation in any other, for there is no other name under heaven given among men by which we must be saved." 13 Now when they saw the boldness of Peter and John, and perceived that they were uneducated and untrained men, they marveled. And they realized that they had been with Jesus. 14 And seeing the man who had been healed standing with them, they could say nothing against it. 15 But when they had commanded them to go aside out of the council, they conferred among themselves, 16 saying, "What shall we do to these men? For, indeed, that a notable miracle has been done through them is evident to all who dwell in Jerusalem, and we cannot deny it. 17 But so that it spreads no further among the people, let us severely threaten them, that from now on they speak to no man in this name." 18 So they called them and commanded them not to speak at all nor teach in the name of Jesus. 19 But Peter and John answered and said to them, "Whether it is right in the sight of God to listen to you more than to God, you judge. 20 For we cannot but speak the things which we have seen and heard." 21 So when they had further threatened them, they let them go, finding no way of punishing them, because of the people, since they all glorified God for what had been done. 22 For the man was over forty years old on whom this miracle of healing had been performed. 23 And being let go, they went to their own companions and reported all that the chief priests and elders had said to them. 24 So when they heard that, they raised their voice to God with one accord and said: "Lord, You are God, who made heaven and earth and the sea, and all that is in them, 25 who by the mouth of Your servant David have said: 'Why did the nations rage, And the people plot vain things? 26 The kings of the earth took their stand, And the rulers were gathered together Against the Lord and against His Christ.' 27 "For truly against Your holy Servant Jesus, whom You anointed, both Herod and Pontius Pilate, with the Gentiles and the people of Israel, were gathered together 28 to do whatever Your hand and Your purpose determined before to be done. 29 Now, Lord, look on their threats, and grant to Your servants that with all boldness they may speak Your word, 30 by stretching out Your hand to heal, and that signs and wonders may be done through the name of Your holy Servant Jesus." 31 And when they had prayed, the place where they were assembled together was shaken; and they were all filled with the Holy Spirit, and they spoke the word of God with boldness. 32 Now the multitude of those who believed were of one heart and one soul; neither did anyone say that any of the things he possessed was his own, but they had all things in common. 33 And with great power the apostles gave witness to the resurrection of the Lord Jesus. And great grace was upon them all. 34 Nor was there anyone among them who lacked; for all who were possessors of lands or houses sold them, and brought the proceeds of the things that were sold, 35 and laid them at the apostles' feet; and they distributed to each as anyone had need. 36 And Joses, who was also named Barnabas by the apostles (which is translated Son of Encouragement), a Levite of the country of Cyprus, 37 having land, sold it, and brought the money and laid it at the apostles' feet.*

INTRODUCTION

A. 'If you can't stand the heat, stay out of the kitchen.' - Harry Truman
B. There will always be opposition to the moving and manifestations of the Holy Spirit.
C. Let's look at Acts 4 to find strength and power so we are able to face and deal with opposition.

I. Facing Opposition

A. The opposition of the Sanhedrin
   1. The people and the priests (as well as the captain of the temple; right hand man of the high priest) the Sanhedrin-Jewish supreme court.
   2. The Sadducees opposed them.
      a. They were wealthy aristocrats.
      b. They did not believe in the resurrection.
      c. They worked with the Romans.
B. How they opposed
   1. These leaders were grieved that they taught on the resurrection of the dead. The priests laid hands on them and put them in custody for the night. 5,000 men (gender specific) were added to the kingdom by believing the word of God.
   2. The next morning these leaders confronted them.
      a. Annas, the high priest, Caiaphas, John, Alexander, rulers, elders, scribes and priests
      b. These were the men who condemned Jesus to death.
      c. The priests put Peter and John in the midst of them. We will be put in the midst of opposition. By what power or name have you done this?
C. Facing the opposition
   1. Face it filled with the Holy Spirit.
      a. Being bold and direct in the name of Jesus of Nazareth and by the resurrection power of God.
      b. The word of God
         i. Peter quoted Psalm 118:22 - ....the stone which was rejected by you builders, which has become the chief cornerstone.
         ii. Isaiah 28:16 - Therefore thus says the Lord GOD: 'Behold, I lay in Zion a stone for a foundation, a tried stone, a precious cornerstone, a sure foundation; whoever believes will not act hastily.'
D. There's no other answer!
   1. Jesus - salvation in no other!
   2. Boldness comes not only from knowing that Jesus saves, but that ONLY JESUS SAVES!
   3. Salvation - soteria - deliverance from sin. Healing health, wholeness!

APPLICATION

1. We all face opposition.
2. II Timothy 3:12 - Yes, and all who desire to live godly in Christ Jesus will suffer persecution.
3. Thank God for opposition. You and I are matured by opposition. It shakes away all that is not built on His foundation. NO COMPROMISE.

II. Dealing With Opposition

A. By being with Jesus.
   1. These priests saw that they were unlearned and ignorant men. They marveled at their boldness.
      a. They had not been trained by the Rabbinical schools.
      b. A Christ-captivated life enables us to live an extraordinary life.
      c. They beheld the healed man and could say nothing!
B. The opposition conferred

    1. What shall we do? That this spreads no further. We must stop them.

    2. They were called and commanded NOT to speak in the NAME OF JESUS!

  C. Opposition brings decisions

    1. They obeyed God. Peter and John said, "Whether it be right in the sight of God to listen to you more than to God, you judge."

      a. I Samuel 15:22 - ". . . .to obey is better than sacrifice. . . ."

      b. We obey God or man.

    2. We must share what we have seen or heard.

      a. Boldness - parresia - telling all. It means conviction, communication and character.

    3. The priests threatened them

      a. But could not punish them

      b. The people glorified God.

      c. The man was over forty years old.

  D. Dealing with opposition in the church

    1. They went back to their companions - the church.

    2. They lifted up their voice to God in one accord with raise, prayer and worship.

    3. Why they prayed:

      a. The Sovereignty of God, (despota—absolute ruler)

      b. Opposition and threats, (Why do the nations rage?)

      c. The assurance God would overrule

      d. That God would give them boldness and confirm His word with signs and wonders

        i. More boldness

        ii. More healings

        iii. More signs, wonders, and miracles

      e. Results!

        i. The place was shaken!

        ii. They were filled with the Holy Spirit

        iii. They spoke the word of God with boldness.

APPLICATION:

  A. How are you dealing with opposition?

  B. Opposition crystallizes boldness.

  C. Difficulties can deepen your determination.

  D. Conflict forces us to clarify our beliefs.

  E. What are you attempting, by God's grace, to do that desperately needs the work of the Holy Spirit to accomplish? BE SPECIFIC!

III. Strength And Power In Opposition

  A. Opposition should bring unity.

    1. One mind and one heart, great power and great grace

    2. They had all things in common. They were committed to Christ and one another.

    3. They had fellowship and communion.

    4. The apostles met the needs as supplies were provided.

  B. Opposition should bring sacrifice

    1. From Joses to Barnabas

    2. He sold land and laid it at the apostle's feet.

    3. We need a Barnabas club! Do you want to join?

APPLICATION: We are a body. We need each other. We need to be committed!

THE CHURCH ON TRIAL

Acts 5 - *But a certain man named Ananias, with Sapphira his wife, sold a possession. 2 And he kept back part of the proceeds, his wife also being aware of it, and brought a certain part and laid it at the apostles' feet. 3 But Peter said, "Ananias, why has Satan filled your heart to lie to the Holy Spirit and keep back part of the price of the land for yourself? 4 While it remained, was it not your own? And after it was sold, was it not in your own control? Why have you conceived this thing in your heart? You have not lied to men but to God." 5 Then Ananias, hearing these words, fell down and breathed his last. So great fear came upon all those who heard these things. 6 And the young men arose and wrapped him up, carried him out, and buried him. 7 Now it was about three hours later when his wife came in, not knowing what had happened. 8 And Peter answered her, "Tell me whether you sold the land for so much?" She said, "Yes, for so much." 9 Then Peter said to her, "How is it that you have agreed together to test the Spirit of the Lord? Look, the feet of those who have buried your husband are at the door, and they will carry you out." 10 Then immediately she fell down at his feet and breathed her last. And the young men came in and found her dead, and carrying her out, buried her by her husband. 11 So great fear came upon all the church and upon all who heard these things. 12 And through the hands of the apostles many signs and wonders were done among the people. And they were all with one accord in Solomon's Porch. 13 Yet none of the rest dared join them, but the people esteemed them highly. 14 And believers were increasingly added to the Lord, multitudes of both men and women, 15 so that they brought the sick out into the streets and laid them on beds and couches, that at least the shadow of Peter passing by might fall on some of them. 16 Also a multitude gathered from the surrounding cities to Jerusalem, bringing sick people and those who were tormented by unclean spirits, and they were all healed. 17 Then the high priest rose up, and all those who were with him (which is the sect of the Sadducees), and they were filled with indignation, 18 and laid their hands on the apostles and put them in the common prison. 19 But at night an angel of the Lord opened the prison doors and brought them out, and said, 20 "Go, stand in the temple and speak to the people all the words of this life." 21 And when they heard that, they entered the temple early in the morning and taught. But the high priest and those with him came and called the council together, with all the elders of the children of Israel, and sent to the prison to have them brought. 22 But when the officers came and did not find them in the prison, they returned and reported, 23 saying, "Indeed we found the prison shut securely, and the guards standing outside before the doors; but when we opened them, we found no one inside!" 24 Now when the high priest, the captain of the temple, and the chief priests heard these things, they wondered what the outcome would be. 25 So one came and told them, saying, "Look, the men whom you put in prison are standing in the temple and teaching the people!" 26 Then the captain went with the officers and brought them without violence, for they feared the people, lest they should be stoned. 27 And when they had brought them, they set them before the council. And the high priest asked them, 28 saying, "Did we not strictly command you not to teach in this name? And look, you have filled Jerusalem with your doctrine, and intend to bring this Man's blood on us!" 29 But Peter and the other apostles answered and said: "We ought to obey God rather than men. 30 The God of our fathers raised up Jesus whom you murdered by hanging on a tree. 31 Him God has exalted to His right hand to be Prince and Savior, to give repentance to Israel and forgiveness of sins. 32 And we are His witnesses to these things, and so also is the Holy Spirit whom God has given to those who obey Him." 33 When they heard this, they were furious and plotted to kill them. 34 Then one in the council stood up, a Pharisee named Gamaliel, a teacher of the law held in respect by all the people, and commanded them to put the apostles outside for a little while. 35 And he said to them: "Men of Israel, take heed to yourselves what you intend to do regarding these men. 36 For some time ago Theudas rose up, claiming to be somebody. A number of men, about four hundred, joined him. He was slain, and all who obeyed him were scattered and came to nothing. 37 After this man, Judas of Galilee rose up in the days of the census, and drew away many people after him. He also perished, and all who obeyed him were dispersed. 38 And now I say to you, keep away from these men and let them alone; for if this plan or this work is of men, it will come to nothing; 39 but if it is of God, you cannot overthrow it—lest you even be found to fight against God." 40 And they agreed with him, and when they had called for the apostles and beaten them, they commanded that they should not speak in the name of Jesus, and let them go. 41 So they departed from the presence of the council, rejoicing that they were counted worthy to suffer shame for His name. 42 And daily in the temple, and in every house, they did not cease teaching and preaching Jesus as the Christ.*

INTRODUCTION

A. "The church's greatest danger has never been created by opposition. When she has been opposed and persecuted she has been pure and strong. Never until she was patronized did she become weak. Wherever the church is patronized and admired by the world she becomes weak." - G. Campbell Morgan.[1] How shall we safeguard against that? WE MUST OBEY GOD.

B. The church is on trial today just as it was then.

C. I Peter 4:12-13 - *Beloved, do not think it strange concerning the fiery trial which is to try you, as though some strange thing happened to you; but rejoice to the extent that you partake of Christ's sufferings, that when His glory is revealed, you may also be glad with exceeding joy.*

D. Let's look at the church on trial and how we can deal with trials in our lives.

I. Open Judgment

A. Ananias on trial.

1. Ananias and his wife sold a piece of property and kept back part of it saying they gave all. They laid it at the apostle's feet.

2. Peter said, "Ananias why has Satan filled your heart so that you have lied to the Holy Spirit and kept back part of the price of the land?"
   a. Satan attempts to fill our hearts the same way he tried with Matthew.
   b. It was Ananias's property to do with what he wanted.
   c. He conceived this idea in his heart and lied to the Holy Spirit.
   d. In this instance we see the gift of discernment in operation.
   e. Ananias falls down, gives up the ghost and great fear was released on all who heard.

3. Sin is judged!
   a. The sin of hypocrisy (mask-wearing)
   b. God will judge sin.
   c. Galatians 6:1 - *Brethren, if a man is overtaken in any trespass, you who are spiritual restore such a one in a spirit of gentleness, considering yourself lest you also be tempted.*
   d. This was an act of discipline; purification of the church.

4. They buried him.

B. Sapphira on trial.

1. Sapphira shows up 3 hours later unaware of what has happened to her husband.

2. She dies.

3. Great fear came on all the church and all that heard.

APPLICATION

A. I Peter 4:17 - *For the time has come for judgment to begin at the house of God; and if it begins with us first, what will be the end of those who do not obey the gospel of God?* May God purify us.

B. Titus 2:14 - *. . . .who gave Himself for us, that He might redeem us from every lawless deed and purify for Himself His own special people, zealous for good works.*

II. Open Power
    A. By the Apostles
        1. Signs and wonders were done. Semeia - outward evidence of the inner working of the power of the Lord in a person or situation.
        2. People did not 'join' the church, they were added. But the people magnified them. Men and women were added to the Lord.
        3. They brought forth the sick out onto the streets and waited for Peter's shadow to fall on them and heal them.
            a. Who is being touched by the shadow of your ministry?
            b. The sick, the demonized, the unclean were healed.
    B. By Us
        1. We are to minister life.
        2. We are to minister healing.

APPLICATION: Who is being touched by your shadow? This is an Eastern phrase meaning people will seek to escape from the evil influence of a man's shadow or get under the good shadow or influence of a good man.

III. Open Opposition
    A. The Sanhedrin opposes.
        1. The Sanhedrin were fill with indignation and threw them in prison.
        2. Their shadow touches people and the enemy seeks to kill them.
    B. God intervenes in opposition.
        1. But the angel of the Lord, by night, opens the prison doors and lets them out.
        2. The angel commands them to go, stand, and speak all the words of this life!
            a. The word life summarized Jesus' ministry and message.
            b. The Lord can open any prison we are in....fear, physical, anger, anxiety.
            c. They taught in the temple.
        3. The Sanhedrin calls for the prisoners.
            a. They found them in the temple. The prison was closed and intact.
            b. They were worried how the church might grow.
            c. "Did we not strictly command you not to teach in this name? And you have filled Jerusalem with your doctrine, and intend to bring this Man's blood on us!"

APPLICATION
    A. In the midst of opposition expect divine intervention!
    B. When he delivers you; go, stand and speak all the words of life.

IV. Open Offensive
    A. We ought to obey God rather than man.
        1. Obedience
        2. They were men of character and principle.
        3. They testified.
            a. The God of our fathers raised Jesus.
            b. They slew Him on the cross.
            c. Him - God exalted to give repentance and forgiveness
            d. We are witnesses by the Holy Spirit.
            e. They were cut to the heart.
    B. God intervenes.
        1. Gamaliel, a Pharisee, a doctor of the law intervenes. (God moves in mysterious ways.)

    2. He gives examples of the Theudas and Judas. He says let them alone. Let God show!
- C. On the offensive again
  1. They beat the Apostles and commanded then not to speak.
  2. Rejoice! They did because they were counted worthy to suffer for His name. Luke 6:22-23 - *Blessed are you when men hate you, and when they exclude you, and revile you, and cast out your name as evil, for the Son of Man's sake.Rejoice in that day and leap for joy! For indeed your reward is great in heaven,for in like manner their fathers did to the prophets.*
  3. And daily in the temple and in every house they ceased not to teach and preach Jesus Christ!

APPLICATION
- A. Overcome evil with good!
- B. The best defense is a good offense!
- C. Overcome by the blood! Revelation 12:11
- D. Overcome by faith. I John 5:4
- E. Trials-patience-experience-hope-love of God. Be offensive! Romans 5:3-5

GROWTH

Acts 6:1-7 - Now in those days, when the number of the disciples was multiplying, there arose a complaint against the Hebrews by the Hellenists, because their widows were neglected in the daily distribution. 2 Then the twelve summoned the multitude of the disciples and said, "It is not desirable that we should leave the word of God and serve tables. 3 Therefore, brethren, seek out from among you seven men of good reputation, full of the Holy Spirit and wisdom, whom we may appoint over this business; 4 but we will give ourselves continually to prayer and to the ministry of the word." 5 And the saying pleased the whole multitude. And they chose Stephen, a man full of faith and the Holy Spirit, and Philip, Prochorus, Nicanor, Timon, Parmenas, and Nicolas, a proselyte from Antioch, 6 whom they set before the apostles; and when they had prayed, they laid hands on them. 7 Then the word of God spread, and the number of the disciples multiplied greatly in Jerusalem, and a great many of the priests were obedient to the faith.

INTRODUCTION

A. Growth involves a price. It causes change. Think how your children have grown!

B. Growth brings problems, as well as being rewarding. Charles Swindoll, "We are all faced with a series of great opportunities brilliantly disguised as impossible situations."

C. Growth in numbers and maturity is God's will for us. Acts shows how God added to and multiplied the early church.

    1. Acts 2:41 - 3,000

    2. Acts 2:47 - More added

    3. Acts 4:4 - 5,000 men

    4. Acts 5:14 - Added

    5. Acts 6:1 - Number of disciples multiplied

    6. Acts 6:7 - Multiplied greatly

D. Let's look at Acts 6 to see how growth brings problems, enlargement and development and how this applies to us.

I. Growth Brings Problems.

A. Growth brought murmuring.

    1. The number of the disciples had multiplied.

    2. The murmuring started.

        a. In the midst of victory there are difficulties.

        b. The occasion was either the actual or supposed neglect of the Hellenist widows regarding the distribution of food.

        c. Most of the widows were probably Hellenists; which were Greek speaking Jews. Many of them were wealthy Jews who had moved back to Jerusalem. There is a possibility that they were the ones who gave the most money to the benevolence fund. Add to this the fact that the apostles were Hebrews.

B. Growth brought more needs. (not apostles)

    1. There is a tendency in human nature to split the fellowship into factions with different apostles. The Hellenists thought the Hebrew Jews were receiving preferential treatment to the Hebrew Jews in the sharing of common things.

    2. The neglect here was widows. We must be careful about neglecting widow, singles, and lonely people. James 1:27 - *Pure and undefiled religion before God and the Father is this: to visit orphans and widows in their trouble, and to keep oneself unspotted from the world.*

    3. We are either part of the problem or part of the solution.

APPLICATION
A. Growth here has caused problems in Acts 6.
B. Growth has caused problems in our church. It will cause problems. Be part of the solution.
C. More needs more opportunities.

II. Growth Brings Enlargement.
A. Enlargement in involvement.
   1. They called the multitude together. They said it is not reasonable that we should leave the word of God to serve tables.
   2. "But we will give ourselves continually to prayer and to the ministry of the Word."
      a. continually - pris-kar-ter-sh-o - to be earnest towards, to persevere, be constantly diligent, continue constant in.
      b. Being in prayer and in the word is powerful. Apostolic prayer will bring apostolic power. The apostles prioritized and enlargement makes us have priorities.
         i. Give time to seeking God. (intimacy)
         ii. Rightly divide the word of truth. II Tim 3:16-17
B. Enlargement happens with help from others.
   1. They said choose seven men with the following.
      a. "men from among you" - Christians
      b. "of good report" - Good witness
      c. "full of the Spirit" - Spirit filled (fruit and power)
      d. "full of wisdom" - James
   2. They chose Hellenist Jews. Stephen, Philip, Prochorus, Nicanor, Timon, Parmenas and Nicolas.
      a. They sought to overcome prejudice. They chose Hellenists to deal with the problem. The church was now bi-cultural.
      b. They laid hands on them and prayed
   3. The result of others helping.
      a. The word of God increased.
      b. The number of disciples multiplied greatly.
      c. A great company of priests were added to the faith.
      d. People were released into their destinies.
      e. From the squabble came a strategy to expand. They became 'more' than deacons.

APPLICATION
A. Growth brings enlargement. The need for involvement is greater.
B. Problems have potential in them.
C. Does your problem have potential in it? Of course! Destiny!

III. Growth Brings Development.
A. Developed Stephen
   1. One of the 'deacons' or servants.
   2. Full of faith and power, wonders and miracles.
   3. It brought opposition in the Greek Synagogue and they had a dispute with Stephen. He was a magnet drawing people but became a moving target.
   4. They were not able to resist the wisdom and the Spirit by which Stephen spoke.
B. Developed Saul (Paul)
   1. Then they caused men to speak falsely against Stephen.
   2. They stirred up the elders and the scribes.
   3. Paul was involved in this. He was there when Stephen died.
   4. They saw the face of Stephen as if it had been the face of an angel.

APPLICATION

A. Enlargement is people like Stephen.

B. Enlargement in potential points out who is now opposing Christians. Growth should be occurring in our lives personally and in opportunities for those 'Paul's' in the future.

C. You will be developed!

STEPHEN

Acts 6:8 - 7:60 - *And Stephen, full of faith and power, did great wonders and signs among the people. 9 Then there arose some from what is called the Synagogue of the Freedmen (Cyrenians, Alexandrians, and those from Cilicia and Asia), disputing with Stephen. 10 And they were not able to resist the wisdom and the Spirit by which he spoke. 11 Then they secretly induced men to say, "We have heard him speak blasphemous words against Moses and God." 12 And they stirred up the people, the elders, and the scribes; and they came upon him, seized him, and brought him to the council. 13 They also set up false witnesses who said, "This man does not cease to speak blasphemous words against this holy place and the law; 14 for we have heard him say that this Jesus of Nazareth will destroy this place and change the customs which Moses delivered to us." 15 And all who sat in the council, looking steadfastly at him, saw his face as the face of an angel. 7:1 Then the high priest said, "Are these things so?" 2 And he said, "Brethren and fathers, listen: The God of glory appeared to our father Abraham when he was in Mesopotamia, before he dwelt in Haran, 3 and said to him, 'Get out of your country and from your relatives, and come to a land that I will show you.' 4 Then he came out of the land of the Chaldeans and dwelt in Haran. And from there, when his father was dead, He moved him to this land in which you now dwell. 5 And God gave him no inheritance in it, not even enough to set his foot on. But even when Abraham had no child, He promised to give it to him for a possession, and to his descendants after him. 6 But God spoke in this way: that his descendants would dwell in a foreign land, and that they would bring them into bondage and oppress them four hundred years. 7 'And the nation to whom they will be in bondage I will judge,' said God, 'and after that they shall come out and serve Me in this place.' 8 Then He gave him the covenant of circumcision; and so Abraham begot Isaac and circumcised him on the eighth day; and Isaac begot Jacob, and Jacob begot the twelve patriarchs. 9 "And the patriarchs, becoming envious, sold Joseph into Egypt. But God was with him 10 and delivered him out of all his troubles, and gave him favor and wisdom in the presence of Pharaoh, king of Egypt; and he made him governor over Egypt and all his house. 11 Now a famine and great trouble came over all the land of Egypt and Canaan, and our fathers found no sustenance. 12 But when Jacob heard that there was grain in Egypt, he sent out our fathers first. 13 And the second time Joseph was made known to his brothers, and Joseph's family became known to the Pharaoh. 14 Then Joseph sent and called his father Jacob and all his relatives to him, seventy-five people. 15 So Jacob went down to Egypt; and he died, he and our fathers. 16 And they were carried back to Shechem and laid in the tomb that Abraham bought for a sum of money from the sons of Hamor, the father of Shechem. 17 "But when the time of the promise drew near which God had sworn to Abraham, the people grew and multiplied in Egypt 18 till another king arose who did not know Joseph. 19 This man dealt treacherously with our people, and oppressed our forefathers, making them expose their babies, so that they might not live. 20 At this time Moses was born, and was well pleasing to God; and he was brought up in his father's house for three months. 21 But when he was set out, Pharaoh's daughter took him away and brought him up as her own son. 22 And Moses was learned in all the wisdom of the Egyptians, and was mighty in words and deeds. 23 "Now when he was forty years old, it came into his heart to visit his brethren, the children of Israel. 24 And seeing one of them suffer wrong, he defended and avenged him who was oppressed, and struck down the Egyptian. 25 For he supposed that his brethren would have understood that God would deliver them by his hand, but they did not understand. 26 And the next day he appeared to two of them as they were fighting, and tried to reconcile them, saying, 'Men, you are brethren; why do you wrong one another?' 27 But he who did his neighbor wrong pushed him away, saying, 'Who made you a ruler and a judge over us? 28 Do you want to kill me as you did the Egyptian yesterday?' 29 Then, at this saying, Moses fled and became a dweller in the land of Midian, where he had two sons. 30 "And when forty years had passed, an Angel of the Lord appeared to him in a flame of fire in a bush, in the wilderness of Mount Sinai. 31 When Moses saw it, he marveled at the sight; and as he drew near to observe, the voice of the Lord came to him, 32 saying, 'I am the God of your fathers—the God of Abraham, the God of Isaac, and the God of Jacob.' And Moses trembled and dared not look. 33 'Then the Lord said to him, "Take your sandals off your feet, for the place where you stand is holy ground. 34 I have surely seen the oppression of My people who are in Egypt; I have heard their groaning and have come down to deliver them. And now come, I will send you to Egypt." ' 35 "This Moses whom they rejected, saying, 'Who made you a ruler and a judge?' is the one God sent to be a ruler and a deliverer by the hand of the Angel who appeared to him in the bush. 36 He brought them out, after he had shown wonders and signs in the land of Egypt, and in the Red Sea, and in the wilderness forty years. 37 "This is that Moses who said to the children of Israel, 'The Lord your God will raise up for you a Prophet like me from your brethren. Him you shall hear.' 38 "This is he who was in the congregation in the wilderness with the Angel who spoke to him on Mount Sinai, and with our fathers, the one who received the living oracles to give to us, 39 whom our fathers would not obey, but rejected. And in their hearts they turned back to Egypt, 40 saying to Aaron, 'Make us gods to go before us; as for this Moses who brought us out of the land of Egypt, we do not know what has become of him.' 41 And they made a calf in those days, offered sacrifices to the idol, and rejoiced in the works of their own hands. 42 Then God turned and gave them up to worship the host of heaven, as it is written in the book of the Prophets: 'Did you offer Me slaughtered animals and sacrifices during forty years in the wilderness, O house of Israel? 43 You also took up the tabernacle of Moloch, And the star of your god Remphan, Images which you made to worship; And I will carry you away beyond Babylon.' 44 "Our fathers had the tabernacle of witness in the wilderness, as He appointed, instructing Moses to make it according to the pattern that he had seen, 45 which our fathers, having received it in turn, also brought with Joshua into the land possessed by the Gentiles, whom God drove out before the face of our fathers until the days of David, 46 who found favor before God and asked to find a dwelling for the God of Jacob. 47 But Solomon built Him a house. 48 "However, the Most High does not dwell in temples made with hands, as the prophet says: 49 'Heaven is My throne, And earth is My footstool. What house will you build for Me? says the Lord, Or what is the place of My rest? 50 Has My hand not made all these things?' Israel Resists the Holy Spirit 51 "You stiff-necked and uncircumcised in heart and ears! You always resist the Holy Spirit; as your fathers did, so do you. 52 Which of the prophets did your fathers not persecute? And they killed those who foretold the coming of the Just One, of whom you now have become the betrayers and murderers, 53 who have received the law by the direction of angels and have not kept it." 54 When they heard these things they were cut to the heart, and they gnashed at him with their teeth. 55 But he, being full of the Holy Spirit, gazed into heaven and saw the glory of God, and Jesus standing at the right hand of God, 56 and said, "Look! I see the heavens opened and the Son of Man standing at the right hand of God!" 57 Then they cried out with a loud voice, stopped their ears, and ran at him with one accord; 58 and they cast him out of the city and stoned him. And the witnesses laid down their clothes at the feet of a young man named Saul. 59 And they stoned Stephen as he was calling on God and saying, "Lord Jesus, receive my spirit." 60 Then he knelt down and cried out with a loud voice, "Lord, do not charge them with this sin." And when he had said this, he fell asleep.*

INTRODUCTION

A. Stephen was full of faith and power and did great signs among the people. (v. 8)
B. The people from the Synagogue of the Freedman (Hellenist Jews) arose and disputed Stephen. (v. 9)
C. They were not able to resist the wisdom and the Spirit by which he spoke! (v. 10)
D. They argue theologically: (vs.11-15)
    1. We heard him speak blasphemes against Moses and God.
    2. They stirred up the people, the elders and scribes and brought him before the crowd.
    3. They set up false witnesses.
    4. They accused Stephen of saying that Jesus of Nazareth was going to destroy the place.
    5. All that looked at Stephen's face said it was as the face of an angel.
E. Let's see what we can learn from Stephen's good example in Acts 6-7.

I. We See That Stephen Stood Strong In The Lord.

A. Standing before the council
    1. "Are these things so?" The high priest asked.

2. Stephen answered and took a stand. Ephesians 6:13 - *Therefore take up the whole armor of God, that you may be able to withstand in the evil day, and having done all, to stand.* He knew what God wanted him to do in this situation.

B. Standing on the Word of God.

1. Abraham
   a. The glory of God appeared to Abraham.
   b. God said, "Get out of your country...."
   c. Romans 4:17-21. God was faithful and gave him Isaac.

   APPLICATION: He went out by faith. He obeyed God's word to him.

2. Joseph
   a. He was sold into Egypt
   b. But God was with him and delivered him out of all his afflictions.
   c. God fulfilled all He had promised Joseph: birth-death-supernatural-fulfillment.

   APPLICATION: God is with us! God speaks through the Word and His encounters with people in history.

1. Moses
   a. By faith Moses was launched out.
   b. He learned all the wisdom of Egypt and was mighty in word and deed.
   c. It came into his heart to visit his brethren. (He was 40 years old) He saw evil and wanted to help but he helped in the wrong way.
   d. 40 years in the wilderness until God visited Moses in the flame of fire in the bush. He was on Holy Ground.
   e. God heard the affliction of the children of Israel.
   f. "Who made you our ruler?" Moses brought them out with signs and wonders.
   g. David and Solomon built a house.
      i. The Most High does not dwell in temples made with hands.
      ii. He has made all. He wants to dwell in our hearts.

   APPLICATION: He forsook the treasures of Egypt esteeming the reproach of Christ's greater riches. He tried to help in his own way. God schooled him and prepared him. He was used to deliver Egypt. God hears the cries of those in bondage. We need to stand on God's Word. We need to obey!

II. We See Stephen Stand As He Saw Christ In The Midst Of The Trial.

A. He preached Christ to them.
   1. He confronted them
      a. "You stiff-necked and uncircumcised in heart and ears."
      b. Jeremiah 4:3-4 - *For thus says the LORD to the men of Judah and Jerusalem: " Break up your fallow ground, and do not sow among thorns.Circumcise yourselves to the LORD, and take away the foreskins of your hearts, you men of Judah and inhabitants of Jerusalem, lest My fury come forth like fire, and burn so that no one can quench it, because of the evil of your doings."*
      c. "You do always resist the Holy Spirit as your fathers did."
      d. They murdered and betrayed Jesus, the Just One.
      e. He convicted them.

B. He saw Christ.
   1. He saw the glory of God and Jesus standing at the right hand of God.
   2. Hebrews 12:1-2
   3. We need to look to Him to draw near to Him.

APPLICATION: I know many of you are standing in difficult trials. He loves you and cares for you. Take steps!

III. We See Stephen Standing In The World.

    A. He shined as a witness.

        1. Matthew 5:16 - *Let your light shine.*

        2. His face shone like an angel.

    B. He forgave them as he stood.

        1. They gnashed their teeth and cried out. They ran at him in one accord.

        2. They stoned him. The penalty for blasphemy. (Deut. 13:6)

        3. He said, "Lord Jesus, receive my spirit. Lay not this sin to their charge." Forgiveness is very important!

        4. Augustine said, "The church owes Paul to the prayer of Stephen."

APPLICATION: He confronted and forgave. He was a bright light for God in the word. Be a light!

THE CHURCH ADVANCING

Acts 8 - Now Saul was consenting to his death. At that time a great persecution arose against the church which was at Jerusalem; and they were all scattered throughout the regions of Judea and Samaria, except the apostles. 2 And devout men carried Stephen to his burial, and made great lamentation over him. 3 As for Saul, he made havoc of the church, entering every house, and dragging off men and women, committing them to prison. 4 Therefore those who were scattered went everywhere preaching the word. 5 Then Philip went down to the city of Samaria and preached Christ to them. 6 And the multitudes with one accord heeded the things spoken by Philip, hearing and seeing the miracles which he did. 7 For unclean spirits, crying with a loud voice, came out of many who were possessed; and many who were paralyzed and lame were healed. 8 And there was great joy in that city. 9 But there was a certain man called Simon, who previously practiced sorcery in the city and astonished the people of Samaria, claiming that he was someone great, 10 to whom they all gave heed, from the least to the greatest, saying, "This man is the great power of God." 11 And they heeded him because he had astonished them with his sorceries for a long time. 12 But when they believed Philip as he preached the things concerning the kingdom of God and the name of Jesus Christ, both men and women were baptized. 13 Then Simon himself also believed; and when he was baptized he continued with Philip, and was amazed, seeing the miracles and signs which were done. 14 Now when the apostles who were at Jerusalem heard that Samaria had received the word of God, they sent Peter and John to them, 15 who, when they had come down, prayed for them that they might receive the Holy Spirit. 16 For as yet He had fallen upon none of them. They had only been baptized in the name of the Lord Jesus. 17 Then they laid hands on them, and they received the Holy Spirit. 18 And when Simon saw that through the laying on of the apostles' hands the Holy Spirit was given, he offered them money, 19 saying, "Give me this power also, that anyone on whom I lay hands may receive the Holy Spirit." 20 But Peter said to him, "Your money perish with you, because you thought that the gift of God could be purchased with money! 21 You have neither part nor portion in this matter, for your heart is not right in the sight of God. 22 Repent therefore of this your wickedness, and pray God if perhaps the thought of your heart may be forgiven you. 23 For I see that you are poisoned by bitterness and bound by iniquity." 24 Then Simon answered and said, "Pray to the Lord for me, that none of the things which you have spoken may come upon me." 25 So when they had testified and preached the word of the Lord, they returned to Jerusalem, preaching the gospel in many villages of the Samaritans. 26 Now an angel of the Lord spoke to Philip, saying, "Arise and go toward the south along the road which goes down from Jerusalem to Gaza." This is desert. 27 So he arose and went. And behold, a man of Ethiopia, a eunuch of great authority under Candace the queen of the Ethiopians, who had charge of all her treasury, and had come to Jerusalem to worship, 28 was returning. And sitting in his chariot, he was reading Isaiah the prophet. 29 Then the Spirit said to Philip, "Go near and overtake this chariot." 30 So Philip ran to him, and heard him reading the prophet Isaiah, and said, "Do you understand what you are reading?" 31 And he said, "How can I, unless someone guides me?" And he asked Philip to come up and sit with him. 32 The place in the Scripture which he read was this: "He was led as a sheep to the slaughter; And as a lamb before its shearer is silent, So He opened not His mouth. 33 In His humiliation His justice was taken away, And who will declare His generation? For His life is taken from the earth." 34 So the eunuch answered Philip and said, "I ask you, of whom does the prophet say this, of himself or of some other man?" 35 Then Philip opened his mouth, and beginning at this Scripture, preached Jesus to him. 36 Now as they went down the road, they came to some water. And the eunuch said, "See, here is water. What hinders me from being baptized?" 37 Then Philip said, "If you believe with all your heart, you may." And he answered and said, "I believe that Jesus Christ is the Son of God." 38 So he commanded the chariot to stand still. And both Philip and the eunuch went down into the water, and he baptized him. 39 Now when they came up out of the water, the Spirit of the Lord caught Philip away, so that the eunuch saw him no more; and he went on his way rejoicing. 40 But Philip was found at Azotus. And passing through, he preached in all the cities till he came to Caesarea.

INTRODUCTION
  A. We are not on a 'retreat', but on an 'advance'. Retreat means going back or backward, or giving up ground before the opposition. Advance means movement forward or toward the front;to go forward as troops.
  B. "The life function of this living organism is to love the God who created it - to care for others out of obedience to Christ, to heal those who hurt, to take away fear, to restore community, to belong to one another, to proclaim the good news while living it out. The church is the invisible made visible."
      - Charles Colson
  C. We must equip people in the church to take Christ into the world. Jesus said, "I will build my church." The church is to be militant and triumphant.
  D. Let's look at how the church advances, where the church advances, and what happens when the church advance. Most importantly I want us to look at how 'we' can advance.

I. **How The Church Advances.**
  A. Persecution
      1. Saul consented to Stephen's death. Stephen was probably buried by faithful Jewish men.
      2. There was great persecution against the church of Jerusalem.
          a. The blood of the martyrs is the seed of the church.
          b. Saul's plan backfired. He probably thought killing Stephen would help halt the Christian movement. Paul had wreaked havoc against the church.In the Greek it means brutal cruelty. A wild animal ravaging a body. He committed them to prison.
      3. They were scattered abroad except the apostles.
          a. The disciples went out. Just as the wind blows seeds a long distance to bear fruit in different places; so does the Holy Spirit scatter the Church and cause them to evangelize the world.
          b. They preached the Word of God everywhere.
          c. The church was established to be mobile.
      4. Problems and persecutions advanced the early Church. (Acts 6 and 8) God raised up men and women to take His message outside the four walls.

APPLICATION: How has God used problems in your life to advance the Gospel? He will send persecution to get us going sometimes.

II. **Where Does God Advance The Church?**
  A. First to Samaria
      1. When the Northern Kingdom fell in 722 BC, many Jews were killed and others carried off to Assyria. Those that intermarried with the Assyrians were called Samaritans.
      2. There was a natural bridge between Jews and Gentiles - Samaritans.
  B. Where Christ was preached!
      1. Philip preached Christ.
      2. The people listened and saw the miracles.
          a. Healings
          b. Deliverance
      3. There was great joy in the city. A great outpouring took place.
      4. Simon the sorcerer "went about claiming to be someone great".
          a. He had deceived and bewitched them with his sorceries.
          b. Christ is preached - The people are delivered when they receive Him.
          c. They were saved and baptized. Philip preached the kingdom of God and the name of Jesus Christ.
  C. Where people go and touch others.

1. Philip arose and went. He left the revival and went into the desert to Gaza.
2. An Ethiopian eunuch, under Candace who was in charge of the treasury, came to Jerusalem to worship.
3. He was sitting in his chariot. The Holy Spirit said to Philip, "Go near and over take this chariot." Is there anyone's chariot near you that God would say to you to join?
    a. "Guidance comes from habitual prayer, Bible study,surrender to be used and openness."[2] - Lloyd Ogilvie
    b. God directs us in many ways.
4. God goes before Philip and prepares the Eunuch.
    a. "How can I unless someone guides me?" the Eunuch commented as he was reading Isaiah. Guide is a technical term for authoritative teaching and interpretation.
    b. Philip preached Jesus and explained Isaiah.
    c. The Eunuch wanted to be water baptized. Philip said, "You can if you believe with all your heart." The Ethiopian said, "I believe that Jesus Christ is the Son of God."
    d. Philip went to his next assignment. He preached in all the cities until he came to Caesarea.
5. God advances His Kingdom where people go and touch others.

APPLICATION: We go to different types of people. We are to preach and live Christ. We go to touch people. Have you "touched someone" or gave yourself away?

III. What Happens When The Church Advances?
   A. People are saved baptized and baptized in the Holy Spirit.
   B. Power encounters.
      1. He made himself to be someone great. The power of God is manifest.
      2. He controlled people.
      3. He tried to buy the power of God.
      4. Peter said, "Your money perish with you. You can't buy the power of God." The apostles told him his heart was not right and that he should repent from this wickedness. The apostles could see that Simon was bound up with iniquity and bitterness. Simon asked for prayer.
      5. They preached in the villages of Samaria.
   C. Other nations are touched.
      1. The Ethiopian Eunuch
      2. Go!

APPLICATION: Lead people to him. Expect encounters and expect God to move. Expect other groups to be saved! He can deliver from bitterness and iniquity. Repent and be forgiven.

SAUL OF TARSUS

Acts 9:1-31 - Then Saul, still breathing threats and murder against the disciples of the Lord, went to the high priest 2 and asked letters from him to the synagogues of Damascus, so that if he found any who were of the Way, whether men or women, he might bring them bound to Jerusalem. 3 As he journeyed he came near Damascus, and suddenly a light shone around him from heaven. 4 Then he fell to the ground, and heard a voice saying to him, "Saul, Saul, why are you persecuting Me?" 5 And he said, "Who are You, Lord?" Then the Lord said, "I am Jesus, whom you are persecuting. It is hard for you to kick against the goads." 6 So he, trembling and astonished, said, "Lord, what do You want me to do?" Then the Lord said to him, "Arise and go into the city, and you will be told what you must do." 7 And the men who journeyed with him stood speechless, hearing a voice but seeing no one. 8 Then Saul arose from the ground, and when his eyes were opened he saw no one. But they led him by the hand and brought him into Damascus. 9 And he was three days without sight, and neither ate nor drank. 10 Now there was a certain disciple at Damascus named Ananias; and to him the Lord said in a vision, "Ananias." And he said, "Here I am, Lord." 11 So the Lord said to him, "Arise and go to the street called Straight, and inquire at the house of Judas for one called Saul of Tarsus, for behold, he is praying. 12 And in a vision he has seen a man named Ananias coming in and putting his hand on him, so that he might receive his sight." 13 Then Ananias answered, "Lord, I have heard from many about this man, how much harm he has done to Your saints in Jerusalem. 14 And here he has authority from the chief priests to bind all who call on Your name." 15 But the Lord said to him, "Go, for he is a chosen vessel of Mine to bear My name before Gentiles, kings, and the children of Israel. 16 For I will show him how many things he must suffer for My name's sake." 17 And Ananias went his way and entered the house; and laying his hands on him he said, "Brother Saul, the Lord Jesus, who appeared to you on the road as you came, has sent me that you may receive your sight and be filled with the Holy Spirit." 18 Immediately there fell from his eyes something like scales, and he received his sight at once; and he arose and was baptized. 19 So when he had received food, he was strengthened. Then Saul spent some days with the disciples at Damascus. 20 Immediately he preached the Christ in the synagogues, that He is the Son of God. 21 Then all who heard were amazed, and said, "Is this not he who destroyed those who called on this name in Jerusalem, and has come here for that purpose, so that he might bring them bound to the chief priests?"

22 But Saul increased all the more in strength, and confounded the Jews who dwelt in Damascus, proving that this Jesus is the Christ. 23 Now after many days were past, the Jews plotted to kill him. 24 But their plot became known to Saul. And they watched the gates day and night, to kill him. 25 Then the disciples took him by night and let him down through the wall in a large basket. 26 And when Saul had come to Jerusalem, he tried to join the disciples; but they were all afraid of him, and did not believe that he was a disciple. 27 But Barnabas took him and brought him to the apostles. And he declared to them how he had seen the Lord on the road, and that He had spoken to him, and how he had preached boldly at Damascus in the name of Jesus. 28 So he was with them at Jerusalem, coming in and going out. 29 And he spoke boldly in the name of the Lord Jesus and disputed against the Hellenists, but they attempted to kill him. 30 When the brethren found out, they brought him down to Caesarea and sent him out to Tarsus. 31 Then the churches throughout all Judea, Galilee, and Samaria had peace and were edified. And walking in the fear of the Lord and in the comfort of the Holy Spirit, they were multiplied.

INTRODUCTION
A. Saul of Tarsus was: (Philippians 2:4-6)
   1. Circumcised the 8th day
   2. Of the stock of Israel

3. Of the tribe of Benjamin
4. A Hebrew of Hebrews
5. As touching the law, a Pharisee
6. Concerning zeal - persecuting the church
7. Touching the righteousness of the law; blameless
B. God desires to intervene in our lives and commune with us.
    1. We have seen the birth and the expansion of the early Church.
    2. Let's look at Saul of Tarsus.

I. Saul Converted

A. Saul was breathing out threats of slaughter against the disciples of the Lord.
    1. He persecuted Christians in Jerusalem. Paul heard that certain Christians escaped to Damascus and he asked for letters to extradite them.
    2. Breathing - emp-neh-o - to inhale, to be animated by (bent upon) breathe
        a. threatening - ap-i-lay - a menace, threatening to forbid - (root)
        b. slaughter - fon-os - to slay, murder, be slain
    3. Saul wanted the Christians bound and brought to Jerusalem.
    4. His anger was so great it was as if he was snorting fire out of his nose.
B. Jesus pursued Saul.
    1. Saul was blinded by a light from heaven while on his way to Damascus.
    2. He fell to the earth and heard a voice saying, "Saul, Saul, why are you persecuting me?"
        a. He was persecuting Christians but Jesus said, "You are persecuting Me!" We are bone of His bone and flesh of His flesh.
        b. Saul asked, "Who are you, Lord?"
    3. The Lord replied, "I am Jesus whom you are persecuting. It is hard for you to Kick against the goads."
        a. Goad: from kenteo, "to prick" denotes - "a sting" - a good or divine impulse, prick, sting. Has the Lord been prodding you?
        b. Saul was beginning to question things, Stephen, etc. God was preparing him.
    4. Saul asked, "Lord, what do You want me to do?"
        a. This is how conversion takes place. Not what do I want, but what do You want me to do, Lord? Not my will but Yours.
        b. The Lord said, "Arise and go into the city, and you will be told what you must do."
            i. He must obey.
            ii. God slays us and then raises us up.
    5. The men with Saul heard a voice but saw no one. He arose and could not see; neither did he eat or drink for three days.
        a. Life begins when we encounter Jesus.
        b. The Lord prepares us for that encounter with the "divine impulse".
        c. Jesus loves us to the end of our resources.

APPLICATION: Jesus is seeking those who are like Saul. He wants to convert them. The Lord alone can open people's hearts. Have you been prodded lately? God might want to visit you.

II. Saul Commissioned

A. Ananias was used.
    1. Ananias was a "certain disciple" in Damascus. Each one of us is a "certain" someone to the Lord. You are special!
    2. God spoke to Ananias in a vision. Ananias said, "Here I am Lord."
        a. Ananias was told to get up and go to a street called Strait and inquire at the house of Judas for Saul.

b. Saul was praying. He was given a vision that Ananias was coming to pray for his sight to be restored.

3. Ananias said, "Lord, I have heard from many about this man, how much harm he has done to your saints in Jerusalem." Saul had the authority to bind up all who called upon the name of Jesus. Ananias must have thought, "Do you know who this is, Lord?"

B. Paul was commissioned.

1. But the Lord said, "Go, for he is a chosen vessel of Mine to bear My name before Gentiles, kings, and the children of Israel. For I will show him how many things he must suffer for My name's sake."

a. Chosen vessel

b. Bear My name.

c. He must suffer for my name's sake.

2. As Ananias placed his hand on Saul he called him "Brother Saul".

a. Saul was healed, filled with the Holy Spirit, and the scales fell off his eyes. He then arose and was baptized.

b. He ate and was strengthened while remaining with the disciples for several days.

APPLICATION: Saul was commissioned. We have been commissioned to do the work of Jesus. We are chosen vessels. We are to bear His Name and we are called to suffer for His Name's sake. You are a "certain disciple" and God wants to use you. He has a plan for each of us!

III. Saul Was Consoled

A. Saul preached Christ.

1. Immediately Saul preached Christ.

2. They were amazed and said, "Is this not he who destroyed those who called on this name in Jerusalem. . . ."

3. He increased in strength and confounded the Jews.

a. I Peter 5:10 - *But may the God of all grace, who called us to His eternal glory by Christ Jesus, after you have suffered a while, perfect, establish, strengthen, and settle you.*

b. Making a stand strengthens us! He proved Jesus is the Christ!

B. The Jews counseled to kill him and they were waiting for him. he disciples took him by night and let him down over a wall in a basket. He was a basket case.

C. Barnabas consoled Saul.

1. Saul tried to join himself with the other disciples, but they were afraid of him.

2. Barnabas brought him to the disciples. Saul shared all the events that had happened from the road to Damascus to Jerusalem.

a. Saul was given Barnabas, the son of consolation or encouragement.

b. "Love thinks no evil." Barnabas did not hold Paul's past against him.

3. The result of Barnabas' actions caused all the churches through Judea, Galilee, and Samaria to be edified and begin walking in the fear of the Lord. These churches were comforted and began to multiply.

APPLICATION: We need Barnabas. We would not have had the Apostle Paul without Barnabas. Saul preached, but was rejected before Barnabas got involved. God confirms His call on our lives through other people.

PETER

Acts 9:31-43 - Then the churches throughout all Judea, Galilee, and Samaria had peace and were edified. And walking in the fear of the Lord and in the comfort of the Holy Spirit, they were multiplied. 32 Now it came to pass, as Peter went through all parts of the country, that he also came down to the saints who dwelt in Lydda. 33 There he found a certain man named Aeneas, who had been bedridden eight years and was paralyzed. 34 And Peter said to him, "Aeneas, Jesus the Christ heals you. Arise and make your bed." Then he arose immediately. 35 So all who dwelt at Lydda and Sharon saw him and turned to the Lord. 36 At Joppa there was a certain disciple named Tabitha, which is translated Dorcas. This woman was full of good works and charitable deeds which she did. 37 But it happened in those days that she became sick and died. When they had washed her, they laid her in an upper room. 38 And since Lydda was near Joppa, and the disciples had heard that Peter was there, they sent two men to him, imploring him not to delay in coming to them. 39 Then Peter arose and went with them. When he had come, they brought him to the upper room. And all the widows stood by him weeping, showing the tunics and garments which Dorcas had made while she was with them. 40 But Peter put them all out, and knelt down and prayed. And turning to the body he said, "Tabitha, arise." And she opened her eyes, and when she saw Peter she sat up. 41 Then he gave her his hand and lifted her up; and when he had called the saints and widows, he presented her alive. 42 And it became known throughout all Joppa, and many believed on the Lord. 43 So it was that he stayed many days in Joppa with Simon, a tanner.

INTRODUCTION

A. Peter the Rock
   1. 'The Christ the Son of the living God.'
   2. The water.
   3. The High Priest's servants ear.
   4. God saw the potential in him.
B. Acts 9:31 - *'Then had the churches rest throughout all Judeo and Galilee and Samaria, and were edified; and walking in the fear of the Lord, and in the comfort of the Holy Ghost, were multiplied.'*
   1. Judea, Galilee, and Samaria had received the Word of God.
   2. They were edified – built up!
   3. They walked in the fear of the Lord – obedience.
   4. The comfort of the Holy Ghost.
C. Let's look at Peter in Acts 9 and how God wants to use us as he used Peter.

I. Peter Ministers Healing

A. Peter ministers with the saints.
   1. The saints of Lydda.
   2. Philip probably preached there after the Ethiopian eunuch. Ministries should build on one another.
B. Peter ministers to a 'certain' man.
   1. We are all certain to the Lord.
   2. His name was Aeneas.
      a. Isaiah 43:1-2 – *But now thus saith the Lord that created thee, O Jacob, and he that formed thee, O Israel, fear not: for I have redeemed thee, I have called thee by thy name; thou art mine. When thou passest through the waters, I will be with thee; and through the rivers, they shall not overflow thee: When thou walkest through the fire, thou shalt not be burned, neither shall the flame kindle up on thee.'*
      b. We are special to God.

3. A man had kept his bed eight years.
   a. People have problems. They need healing.
   b. He had palsy.
   c. Jesus Christ, Aeneas. Jesus Christ makes you whole. Arise and make your bed. She arose immediately and all at Lydda and Saron saw him and turned to the Lord.
   d. He was led of the Holy Spirit. John 5:19-20.
4. People turn to the Lord when they see people healed and saved.
   a. Healing and evangelism.
   b. God moves by His power.

APPLICATION: We are to minister healing to people in Jesus name. He is the one that makes people whole.

II. Peter Ministers Life
A. Tabitha showed the life of Jesus.
   1. Dorcas
   2. This woman was full of good works and almsdeeds which she did.
      a. She was a doer of the Word.
      b. She used her ministry. She made garments for the poor.
      c. She had the gift of helps.
      d. Use what God has given you.
B. Peter ministers life in death.
   1. Dorcas or Tabitha was sick and died. They laid her in the upper chamber.
   2. Peter went to Joppa. Peter put them all out. He prayed and said, Arise. And she opened her eyes: and when he had called the saints and widows.
   3. We need to minister life in Jesus name.
      a. Proverbs 18:21 – *Death and life are in the power of the tongue: and they that love it shall eat the fruit thereof.*
      b. John 10:10 - ...*life more abundantly.*

APPLICATION: We are the minister life. LIFE IN JESUS NAME! LIFE IN DEATH!!

III. Peter Ministers New Wine
A. Peter breaks barriers.
   1. He went to Simon the Tanner.
   2. Jews abhorred Tanners.
   3. We will have to break down barriers.
B. Peter allowed the Holy Spirit to work in Him.
   1. Mark 2:21-22 – *No man soweth a piece of cloth on an old garment: else the new piece that filled it up taketh away from the old, and the rent is made worse. And no man putteth new wine into old bottles: else the new wine doth burst the bottles, and the wine is spilled, and the bottles will be? But new wine must be put into new bottles.*
   2. Let God do a new thing in your life.

APPLICATION: God will break down barriers. He will put new wine into new wineskins.

THE EXPANSION OF THE KINGDOM OF GOD

Acts 10 - There was a certain man in Caesarea called Cornelius, a centurion of what was called the Italian Regiment, 2 a devout man and one who feared God with all his household, who gave alms generously to the people, and prayed to God always. 3 About the ninth hour of the day he saw clearly in a vision an angel of God coming in and saying to him, "Cornelius!" 4 And when he observed him, he was afraid, and said, "What is it, lord?" So he said to him, "Your prayers and your alms have come up for a memorial before God. 5 Now send men to Joppa, and send for Simon whose surname is Peter. 6 He is lodging with Simon, a tanner, whose house is by the sea. He will tell you what you must do." 7 And when the angel who spoke to him had departed, Cornelius called two of his household servants and a devout soldier from among those who waited on him continually. 8 So when he had explained all these things to them, he sent them to Joppa. 9 The next day, as they went on their journey and drew near the city, Peter went up on the housetop to pray, about the sixth hour. 10 Then he became very hungry and wanted to eat; but while they made ready, he fell into a trance 11 and saw heaven opened and an object like a great sheet bound at the four corners, descending to him and let down to the earth. 12 In it were all kinds of four-footed animals of the earth, wild beasts, creeping things, and birds of the air. 13 And a voice came to him, "Rise, Peter; kill and eat." 14 But Peter said, "Not so, Lord! For I have never eaten anything common or unclean." 15 And a voice spoke to him again the second time, "What God has cleansed you must not call common." 16 This was done three times. And the object was taken up into heaven again. 17 Now while Peter wondered within himself what this vision which he had seen meant, behold, the men who had been sent from Cornelius had made inquiry for Simon's house, and stood before the gate. 18 And they called and asked whether Simon, whose surname was Peter, was lodging there. 19 While Peter thought about the vision, the Spirit said to him, "Behold, three men are seeking you. 20 Arise therefore, go down and go with them, doubting nothing; for I have sent them." 21 Then Peter went down to the men who had been sent to him from Cornelius, and said, "Yes, I am he whom you seek. For what reason have you come?" 22 And they said, "Cornelius the centurion, a just man, one who fears God and has a good reputation among all the nation of the Jews, was divinely instructed by a holy angel to summon you to his house, and to hear words from you." 23 Then he invited them in and lodged them. On the next day Peter went away with them, and some brethren from Joppa accompanied him. 24 And the following day they entered Caesarea. Now Cornelius was waiting for them, and had called together his relatives and close friends. 25 As Peter was coming in, Cornelius met him and fell down at his feet and worshiped him. 26 But Peter lifted him up, saying, "Stand up; I myself am also a man." 27 And as he talked with him, he went in and found many who had come together. 28 Then he said to them, "You know how unlawful it is for a Jewish man to keep company with or go to one of another nation. But God has shown me that I should not call any man common or unclean. 29 Therefore I came without objection as soon as I was sent for. I ask, then, for what reason have you sent for me?" 30 So Cornelius said, "Four days ago I was fasting until this hour; and at the ninth hour I prayed in my house, and behold, a man stood before me in bright clothing, 31 and said, 'Cornelius, your prayer has been heard, and your alms are remembered in the sight of God. 32 Send therefore to Joppa and call Simon here, whose surname is Peter. He is lodging in the house of Simon, a tanner, by the sea. When he comes, he will speak to you.' 33 So I sent to you immediately, and you have done well to come. Now therefore, we are all present before God, to hear all the things commanded you by God." 34 Then Peter opened his mouth and said: "In truth I perceive that God shows no partiality. 35 But in every nation whoever fears Him and works righteousness is accepted by Him. 36 The word which God sent to the children of Israel, preaching peace through Jesus Christ—He is Lord of all— 37 that word you know, which was proclaimed throughout all Judea, and began from Galilee after the baptism which John preached: 38 how God anointed Jesus of Nazareth with the Holy Spirit and with power, who went about doing good and healing all who were oppressed by the devil, for God was with Him. 39 And we are witnesses of all things which He did both in the land of the Jews and in Jerusalem, whom they killed by hanging on a tree. 40 Him God raised up on the third day, and showed Him openly, 41 not to all the people, but to witnesses chosen before by God, even to us who ate and drank with Him after He arose from the dead. 42 And He commanded us to preach to the people, and to testify that it is He who was ordained by God to be Judge of the living and the dead. 43 To Him all the prophets witness that, through His name, whoever believes in Him will receive remission of sins." 44 While Peter was still speaking these words, the Holy Spirit fell upon all those who heard the word. 45 And [o]those of the circumcision who believed were astonished, as many as came with Peter, because the gift of the Holy Spirit had been poured out on the Gentiles also. 46 For they heard them speak with tongues and magnify God. Then Peter answered, 47 "Can anyone forbid water, that these should not be baptized who have received the Holy Spirit just as we have?" 48 And he commanded them to be baptized in the name of the Lord. Then they asked him to stay a few days.

INTRODUCTION

A. We left Peter at Simon the Tanner's house last week.

B. In order to understand the miracle of the conversion of Cornelius, we need to understand some things. The "Christian Movement" was almost exclusively Hebrew. Up to this point there had been some Gentile influence. No orthodox Jew would ever enter the house of a Gentile or a God-fearer. A God-fearer enjoyed a special place in their synagogue communities.

C. The Kingdom of God:

    a. Basileia in Greek means kingship or royal rule.

    b. The Kingdom of God is the rule and reign of Christ.

D. Let's look at the expansion of the Kingdom & how God wants to use us to expand His Kingdom!

I. The Vision Of Expanding The Kingdom Of God

A. The vision of Cornelius

    1. There was a certain man in Caesarea called Cornelius.

        a. A centurion stationed at Caesarea

        b. Of the Italian Regiment - Roman Army

        c. A devout man - disciplined

        d. a God-fearer with all his house - a Gentile that had joined themselves to the Jewish religion.

        e. He gave alms - He was a man of love and kindness

        f. He prayed. Matthew 7:7,8 - *Ask, and it will be given to you; seek, and you will find; knock, and it will be opened to you. For everyone who asks receives, and he who seeks finds, and to him who knocks it will be opened.*

    2. He saw a vision.

        a. At the ninth hour - 3pm in the afternoon. The usual Jewish hour of prayer.

        b. He saw an angel of God coming to him.

        c. The angel said, "Cornelius!" Cornelius responded, "What is it lord?" He was afraid. "Your prayers and alms have come up to God as a memorial."

            i. Revelation 8:4,5 - *"And the smoke of the incense, with the prayers of the saints, ascended before God from the angel's hand. Then the angel took the censer, filled it with fire from the altar, and threw it to the earth. And there were noises, thunderings, lightnings, and an earthquake."*

            ii. Memorial - mnemosyna - a reminder, memorandum, record. Vines - denotes a memorial, that which keeps alive. The memory of someone or something.

        d. He gave him instructions to send men to Joppa to Simon the Tanner to see Peter. In Acts 11:14 - "[Peter] who will tell you words by which you and all your household will be saved."

        e. Joel 2:28-30 - *And I will pour out...*

    3. He obeyed the vision.

a. The angel departed. Cornelius sent two servants and a devout soldier to Joppa to Simon.

b. Acts 26:19 - *Therefore, King Agrippa, I was not disobedient to the heavenly vision....*

APPLICATION: God wants to give us a vision to expand His Kingdom. Be open. Cornelius was in the place of prayer.

    B. The vision of Peter.
        1. Peter went to pray.
            a. The sixth hour = noon
            b. He was hungry when he fell into a trance.
        2. Peter saw a vision.
            a. Heaven opened.
            b. Peter saw a sheet bound at four corners filled with all kinds of beasts and fowl.
            c. A voice came to Peter, "Rise, kill and eat."
            d. Peter said, "Not so, Lord!" The second time the voice said, "What God has cleansed do not call common."
                i. You are not common. You are cleansed.
                ii. You are special.
                iii. God wants all men to be saved.
            e. This scene took place three times before the sheet was taken back to heaven.
        3. Peter had help.
            a. Peter doubted what this meant. While he thought on the vision, the men that Cornelius sent arrived.
            b. While he thought = dienthamoumenou - a double compound - he revolved the truths over and over in his mind. The Spirit said, "Behold, three men seek you...."
            c. They lodged with Peter and Simon the Tanner.
                i. Prejudice was beginning to break down.
                ii. God spoke in parabolic fashion to Peter.

APPLICATION
    A. The Lord often follows a concept with an experience in which our thinking and behavior can be altered by choosing the truth.
    B. First, the Lord seeks to create a willingness. Second, a thought and truth out of Scripture. Third, through relationships and responsibilities.
    C. St. Bernard said, "Draw me, however unwilling to make me willing, draw me, slow-footed, to make me run."
    D. It was easier for Him to get through to Cornelius, the God-fearer than Peter, the apostle.
    E. God is specific: The angel knew Cornelius' name and his petitions to God. He also knew the two names of Peter and his exact location.

II. The Fulfillment Of The Vision Of The Expansion Of The Kingdom Of God
    A. Cornelius' fulfillment
        1. Cornelius saw Peter
            a. Cornelius worshiped Peter. Peter said, "Stand up...." Humility will advance the kingdom.
            b. God showed Peter that it was not unlawful to keep company with a Gentile. God showed him he should call no man common or unclean.
        2. Cornelius told Peter of the vision. Cornelius sent for him to come in fulfillment to the vision of God.

APPLICATION: God fulfills when He rules and reigns.

B. Peter's fulfillment
  1. Peter perceived and preached
     a. "In truth I perceive that God shows no partiality. But in every nation whoever fears Him and works righteousness is accepted by Him."
     b. The word is Jesus - He is Lord of all. Peace by Him.
     c. It began after John the Baptist was in Jordan and Galilee.
     d. God anointed Jesus of Nazareth with the Holy Spirit and power. To: 1) Do good 2) Heal those oppressed of the devil.
     e. We are witnesses of the Cross, the Resurrection, chosen by Him, commanded to preach that He is ordained of God.

APPLICATION: Peter preached to the unclean, that are now clean. He proclaimed Jesus! Advance and expand His Kingdom by doing good and healing those oppressed of the devil.

  2. The Holy Spirit fulfillment
     a. Peter began his message but was interrupted.
     b. The Holy Spirit fell on them which heard the word. Preach the word.
     c. The Jews were astonished because the Gentiles had the Holy Spirit poured out on them. They heard them speak in tongues and magnify God.
     d. Peter said, "Can anyone forbid them from being baptized in water?"
     e. He stayed several days.

APPLICATION: The Lord expanded His Kingdom in power, salvation, baptism with the Holy Spirit, and baptism in water. Acts 10:38 Are you saved?

WHO WAS I, THAT I COULD WITHSTAND GOD?

Acts 11 - Now the apostles and brethren who were in Judea heard that the Gentiles had also received the word of God. 2 And when Peter came up to Jerusalem, those of the circumcision contended with him, 3 saying, "You went in to uncircumcised men and ate with them!" 4 But Peter explained it to them in order from the beginning, saying: 5 "I was in the city of Joppa praying; and in a trance I saw a vision, an object descending like a great sheet, let down from heaven by four corners; and it came to me. 6 When I observed it intently and considered, I saw four-footed animals of the earth, wild beasts, creeping things, and birds of the air. 7 And I heard a voice saying to me, 'Rise, Peter; kill and eat.' 8 But I said, 'Not so, Lord! For nothing common or unclean has at any time entered my mouth.' 9 But the voice answered me again from heaven, 'What God has cleansed you must not call common.' 10 Now this was done three times, and all were drawn up again into heaven. 11 At that very moment, three men stood before the house where I was, having been sent to me from Caesarea. 12 Then the Spirit told me to go with them, doubting nothing. Moreover these six brethren accompanied me, and we entered the man's house. 13 And he told us how he had seen an angel standing in his house, who said to him, 'Send men to Joppa, and call for Simon whose surname is Peter, 14 who will tell you words by which you and all your household will be saved.' 15 And as I began to speak, the Holy Spirit fell upon them, as upon us at the beginning. 16 Then I remembered the word of the Lord, how He said, 'John indeed baptized with water, but you shall be baptized with the Holy Spirit.' 17 If therefore God gave them the same gift as He gave us when we believed on the Lord Jesus Christ, who was I that I could withstand God?" 18 When they heard these things they became silent; and they glorified God, saying, "Then God has also granted to the Gentiles repentance to life." 19 Now those who were scattered after the persecution that arose over Stephen traveled as far as Phoenicia, Cyprus, and Antioch, preaching the word to no one but the Jews only. 20 But some of them were men from Cyprus and Cyrene, who, when they had come to Antioch, spoke to the Hellenists, preaching the Lord Jesus. 21 And the hand of the Lord was with them, and a great number believed and turned to the Lord. 22 Then news of these things came to the ears of the church in Jerusalem, and they sent out Barnabas to go as far as Antioch. 23 When he came and had seen the grace of God, he was glad, and encouraged them all that with purpose of heart they should continue with the Lord. 24 For he was a good man, full of the Holy Spirit and of faith. And a great many people were added to the Lord. 25 Then Barnabas departed for Tarsus to seek Saul. 26 And when he had found him, he brought him to Antioch. So it was that for a whole year they assembled with the church and taught a great many people. And the disciples were first called Christians in Antioch. 27 And in these days prophets came from Jerusalem to Antioch. 28 Then one of them, named Agabus, stood up and showed by the Spirit that there was going to be a great famine throughout all the world, which also happened in the days of Claudius Caesar. 29 Then the disciples, each according to his ability, determined to send relief to the brethren dwelling in Judea. 30 This they also did, and sent it to the elders by the hands of Barnabas and Saul.

INTRODUCTION
A. This story is told twice showing its importance. Luke, the author of Acts, saw this as a milestone.
B. "Man will have his say, but God will have His way."
C. We need to be open to God.
D. Let's look at how Peter, the Apostles, Barnabas, and Agabus did not withstand God and how we should not either.

I. Peter And The Apostles Did Not Withstand God.
A. The Apostles heard about Peter and confronted him.

1. The Apostles and brethren in Judea heard that the Gentiles had received the Word of God.
2. In Jerusalem they practiced circumcision. Because of this there were those who contended with Peter for going into the home of uncircumcised Gentiles and eating with them.
   a. Proverbs 29:25 - *The fear of man brings a snare, but whoever trusts in the Lord shall be safe.*
   b. Proverbs 9:10 - *The fear of the Lord is the beginning of wisdom, and the knowledge of the Holy One is understanding.*

B. Peter explained his actions.
1. He had rehearsed it. He was prepared and gave just the facts.
2. He told them about the vision he received during prayer. "What God has cleansed you must not call common."
3. He told them the story of Cornelius.
4. Verse 14 - . . . .*who will tell you words by which you and all your household will be saved.*
   a. The Holy Spirit fell on them.
   b. God gave them the same gift. Gift=free gift.
   c. The proof of Christianity is the resurrection of Christ and that it works in men's lives.
5. ". . . .who was I that I could withstand God?"

APPLICATION: Are you withstanding God? Repent and receive the gift of eternal life. I John 5:11-13. Lloyd Ogilvie - "There's a great difference between having the Lord on our agenda and being on His." Be open to God. One place the Lord does not want us to stay is where we are - GROW!

II. Barnabas And Saul Did Not Withstand God.

A. First, those scattered preached the Word.
1. The persecution Saul helped to start caused the people to preach the Gospel and expand God's kingdom.
2. These men preached and God's hand was with them and a great number believed and turned to the Lord. Antioch was the third greatest city in the world next to Rome and Alexandria and famous for her chariot-racing And the pursuit of pleasure. They worshipped Daphne - the goddess of immorality.

B. Second, Barnabas is sent to minister.
1. They sent Barnabas to Antioch. Barnabas loved and cared for people.
2. "When he came and had seen the grace of God, he was glad, and encouraged them all that with purpose of heart they should continue with the Lord." He was full of the Holy Spirit and many people were saved.
   a. Titus 2:11-15
   b. Ephesians 2:8,9
   c. Cling to God.
   d. Exhorted—comfort, encourage.

C. Thirdly, he went to get Saul
1. Barnabas went and hunted for him. Saul was perfect for the job - intellectual training, Roman citizenship, spiritual power, to establish God's beachhead. He responded and we have the first missionary team. God prepared Saul for about nine years. Is He preparing you?
2. They taught for a year in Antioch. The disciples were called Christians. The people of Antioch came to realize that they were Christ-like in nature leaving behind their exclusive Hebrew tendencies.

APPLICATION: Don't withstand God's preparation! Use the gifts he has given you. We see evangelism, the apostle, the prophet, the pastor, and the teacher. It is good to be teamed up with others.

III. Agabus And Antioch Did Not Withstand God.
    A. Agabus prophesied as God led him.
        1. A New Testament prophet that fore-told of a famine that would go throughout the world.
        2. He "stood" up for Jesus.
    B. Antioch gave as "Christians".
        1. They sent an offering and every man gave according to his ability.
        2. No wonder they were Christians - "giving".

APPLICATION: Don't withstand God. Agabus was used to speak. Don't withstand God in the area of giving!!

BOOK OF ACTS SERIES | LESSON 15
THE CHRISTIAN LIFE
(or Struck by an Angel)

Acts 12 - Now about that time Herod the king stretched out his hand to harass some from the church. 2 Then he killed James the brother of John with the sword. 3 And because he saw that it pleased the Jews, he proceeded further to seize Peter also. Now it was during the Days of Unleavened Bread. 4 So when he had arrested him, he put him in prison, and delivered him to four squads of soldiers to keep him, intending to bring him before the people after Passover. 5 Peter was therefore kept in prison, but constant prayer was offered to God for him by the church. 6 And when Herod was about to bring him out, that night Peter was sleeping, bound with two chains between two soldiers; and the guards before the door were keeping the prison. 7 Now behold, an angel of the Lord stood by him, and a light shone in the prison; and he struck Peter on the side and raised him up, saying, "Arise quickly!" And his chains fell off his hands. 8 Then the angel said to him, "Gird yourself and tie on your sandals"; and so he did. And he said to him, "Put on your garment and follow me." 9 So he went out and followed him, and did not know that what was done by the angel was real, but thought he was seeing a vision. 10 When they were past the first and the second guard posts, they came to the iron gate that leads to the city, which opened to them of its own accord; and they went out and went down one street, and immediately the angel departed from him. 11 And when Peter had come to himself, he said, "Now I know for certain that the Lord has sent His angel, and has delivered me from the hand of Herod and from all the expectation of the Jewish people." 12 So, when he had considered this, he came to the house of Mary, the mother of John whose surname was Mark, where many were gathered together praying. 13 And as Peter knocked at the door of the gate, a girl named Rhoda came to answer. 14 When she recognized Peter's voice, because of her gladness she did not open the gate, but ran in and announced that Peter stood before the gate. 15 But they said to her, "You are beside yourself!" Yet she kept insisting that it was so. So they said, "It is his angel." 16 Now Peter continued knocking; and when they opened the door and saw him, they were astonished. 17 But motioning to them with his hand to keep silent, he declared to them how the Lord had brought him out of the prison. And he said, "Go, tell these things to James and to the brethren." And he departed and went to another place. 18 Then, as soon as it was day, there was no small stir among the soldiers about what had become of Peter. 19 But when Herod had searched for him and not found him, he examined the guards and commanded that they should be put to death. And he went down from Judea to Caesarea, and stayed there. 20 Now Herod had been very angry with the people of Tyre and Sidon; but they came to him with one accord, and having made Blastus the king's personal aide their friend, they asked for peace, because their country was supplied with food by the king's country. 21 So on a set day Herod, arrayed in royal apparel, sat on his throne and gave an oration to them. 22 And the people kept shouting, "The voice of a god and not of a man!" 23 Then immediately an angel of the Lord struck him, because he did not give glory to God. And he was eaten by worms and died. 24 But the word of God grew and multiplied. 25 And Barnabas and Saul returned from Jerusalem when they had fulfilled their ministry, and they also took with them John whose surname was Mark.

INTRODUCTION

A. The Christian life in the book of Acts is full of surprises and changes. Barnabas and Paul are on their way back to Jerusalem to bring the offering from Antioch.

B. They have seen salvations, healings and deliverances, but they have also experienced persecution and opposition.

C. There is a tension between the beauty and glory of God's eternal kingdom and the ever-present forces of darkness.

D. Let's look at he Christian life and how we can deal with the problems of imprisonment, how we can have the power of intercession and see the punishment of iniquity.

I. The Problems Of Imprisonment

A. This is the story of Peter's miraculous escape from prison. It is also the story of James' martyrdom. James died in faith. Peter was delivered in faith.
   1. Herod Agrippa I was the nephew of Herod Antipas who had murdered John the Baptist. Herod had been educated in Rome, but he kept the law and Jewish observances to remain in good graces with the Jewish people.
   2. Great persecution broke out on the church, especially toward the leaders.
B. The supreme evidence of faith is we retain our integrity in God's ability and faithfulness.
C. There was a great battle going on in the spiritual realm here. Great precautions were made to make sure Peter did not escape. He was guarded by four squads (tetrads-squads of four) or sixteen guards. He was chained by two hands instead of one.
D. Many of us have experienced imprisonment. Many might be living in prison now.
   1. Some people are imprisoned by their past. They will not forget their sinful past and will not forgive themselves for what happened.
   2. Some people are imprisoned by the unforgiveness of others and are bound to that person for life.
   3. Some people are imprisoned by the present. Unable to deal with present situations, because of the deceitfulness of sin.
   4. Some people are imprisoned to habits, fears, etc....
   5. Christ has come to set the captive free!
      a. John 8:31-32 - *Then Jesus said to those Jews who believed Him, "If you abide in My word, you are My disciples indeed. And you shall know the truth, and the truth shall make you free."*
      b. John 8:36 - *Therefore if the Son makes you free, you shall be free indeed.*
   6. We build walls to protect ourselves sometimes; this is imprisonment.
   7. Satan attempts to arrest and imprison us. Jesus sets us free!

II. The Power Of Intercession.

A. Peter was in prison and the church constantly prayed for him. It was intense, constant prayer.
B. God wants to work with us and through us. He has chosen prayer as the vehicle.
C. To intercede means to act as a go-between. Moses interceded for Israel. Abraham interceded for Lot. Christ is interceding for us! Romans 8. We do not know how to pray but the Holy Spirit does!
D. They probably prayed day and night. The angel struck the apostle and told him to arise. He told him to get his shoes and coat on and come with him. Peter thought it was a vision. When they got outside the prison he knew what had happened. He came to his senses. The Lord delivered him. Hebrews says the angels are sent to minister to the heirs of salvation.
E. He ran to the home of Barnabas' aunt; the mother of John, Mark and Mary.
F. James 5:16 - ....*the effective, fervent prayer of a righteous man avails much*
G. Peter knocked on the door and a young girl heard his voice and told them Peter was there. They said it must be his angel.
H. Peter knocked continually until they finally opened the door.
   1. It is possible our answer to prayer is knocking on the door?
   2. Expect and receive. Colossians 4:2 - *Continue earnestly in prayer, being vigilant in it with thanksgiving...*
   3. One problem we often face is not how pray but what to pray. Discouragement over what we perceived as unanswered prayer in the past should not stop us now.
   4. Listen carefully, ask boldly, pray scripturally, trust completely and know the answer is part of God's bigger plan.

5. One man said, "While I was praying, expecting very little, God had already done something great, so great that I had a hard time accepting the answer. God does have a sense of humor doesn't he? The answer was there, but they did not believe it!

6. May we learn the power of intercessory prayer.

APPLICATION
A. Pray expecting.
B. Hebrews 11:6 - *But without faith it is impossible to please Him, for he who comes to God must believe that He is, and that He is a rewarder of those who diligently seek Him.*
C. Your prayers make a difference!

III. The Punishment Of Iniquity
A. God keeps the books, and the battle is the Lord's. The guards were killed for letting Peter go.
B. We will be persecuted. The servant is greater than His Lord. James had already drank his cup and had been baptized with His baptism.
C. Vengeance is the Lord's.
D. The church was not demonstrating against Herod, but God showed whose side He was on.
E. In a festival, bringing peace with Tyre and Sidon. The people cried out about Herod. "The voice of a god and not of a man! Then immediately an angel of the Lord struck him, because he did not give glory to God."
F. God's word grows and multiplies during persecution. God takes care of the church. Barnabas, Saul and John Mark fulfilled His kingdom.

APPLICATION:
A. God will advance His kingdom.
B. Be released from your prison.
C. Pray in powerful intercession.
D. The Christian life is full of excitement and trials!
E. "The chapter opens with James dead, Peter in prison, and Herod triumphing. It closes with Herod dead, Peter free, and the Word of God triumphing." - John Stott

MISSION

Acts 13 - *Now in the church that was at Antioch there were certain prophets and teachers: Barnabas, Simeon who was called Niger, Lucius of Cyrene, Manaen who had been brought up with Herod the tetrarch, and Saul. 2 As they ministered to the Lord and fasted, the Holy Spirit said, "Now separate to Me Barnabas and Saul for the work to which I have called them." 3 Then, having fasted and prayed, and laid hands on them, they sent them away. 4 So, being sent out by the Holy Spirit, they went down to Seleucia, and from there they sailed to Cyprus. 5 And when they arrived in Salamis, they preached the word of God in the synagogues of the Jews. They also had John as their assistant. 6 Now when they had gone through the island to Paphos, they found a certain sorcerer, a false prophet, a Jew whose name was Bar-Jesus, 7 who was with the proconsul, Sergius Paulus, an intelligent man. This man called for Barnabas and Saul and sought to hear the word of God. 8 But Elymas the sorcerer (for so his name is translated) withstood them, seeking to turn the proconsul away from the faith. 9 Then Saul, who also is called Paul, filled with the Holy Spirit, looked intently at him 10 and said, "O full of all deceit and all fraud, you son of the devil, you enemy of all righteousness, will you not cease perverting the straight ways of the Lord? 11 And now, indeed, the hand of the Lord is upon you, and you shall be blind, not seeing the sun for a time." And immediately a dark mist fell on him, and he went around seeking someone to lead him by the hand. 12 Then the proconsul believed, when he saw what had been done, being astonished at the teaching of the Lord. 13 Now when Paul and his party set sail from Paphos, they came to Perga in Pamphylia; and John, departing from them, returned to Jerusalem. 14 But when they departed from Perga, they came to Antioch in Pisidia, and went into the synagogue on the Sabbath day and sat down. 15 And after the reading of the Law and the Prophets, the rulers of the synagogue sent to them, saying, "Men and brethren, if you have any word of exhortation for the people, say on." 16 Then Paul stood up, and motioning with his hand said, "Men of Israel, and you who fear God, listen: 17 The God of this people Israel chose our fathers, and exalted the people when they dwelt as strangers in the land of Egypt, and with an uplifted arm He brought them out of it. 18 Now for a time of about forty years He put up with their ways in the wilderness. 19 And when He had destroyed seven nations in the land of Canaan, He distributed their land to them by allotment. 20 "After that He gave them judges for about four hundred and fifty years, until Samuel the prophet. 21 And afterward they asked for a king; so God gave them Saul the son of Kish, a man of the tribe of Benjamin, for forty years. 22 And when He had removed him, He raised up for them David as king, to whom also He gave testimony and said, 'I have found David the son of Jesse, a man after My own heart, who will do all My will.' 23 From this man's seed, according to the promise, God raised up for Israel a Savior—Jesus— 24 after John had first preached, before His coming, the baptism of repentance to all the people of Israel. 25 And as John was finishing his course, he said, 'Who do you think I am? I am not He. But behold, there comes One after me, the sandals of whose feet I am not worthy to loose.' 26 "Men and brethren, sons of the family of Abraham, and those among you who fear God, to you the word of this salvation has been sent. 27 For those who dwell in Jerusalem, and their rulers, because they did not know Him, nor even the voices of the Prophets which are read every Sabbath, have fulfilled them in condemning Him. 28 And though they found no cause for death in Him, they asked Pilate that He should be put to death. 29 Now when they had fulfilled all that was written concerning Him, they took Him down from the tree and laid Him in a tomb. 30 But God raised Him from the dead. 31 He was seen for many days by those who came up with Him from Galilee to Jerusalem, who are His witnesses to the people. 32 And we declare to you glad tidings—that promise which was made to the fathers. 33 God has fulfilled this for us their children, in that He has raised up Jesus. As it is also written in the second Psalm: 'You are My Son, today I have begotten You.' 34 And that He raised Him from the dead, no more to return to corruption, He has spoken thus: 'I will give you the sure mercies of David.' 35 Therefore He also says in another Psalm: 'You will not allow Your Holy One to see corruption.' 36 "For David, after he had served his own generation by the will of God, fell asleep, was buried with his fathers, and saw corruption; 37 but He whom God raised up saw no corruption. 38 Therefore let it be known to you, brethren, that through this Man is preached to you the forgiveness of sins; 39 and by Him everyone who believes is justified from all things from which you could not be justified by the law of Moses. 40 Beware therefore, lest what has been spoken in the prophets come upon you: 41 'Behold, you despisers, Marvel and perish! For I work a work in your days, a work which you will by no means believe, though one were to declare it to you.' " 42 So when the Jews went out of the synagogue, the Gentiles begged that these words might be preached to them the next Sabbath. 43 Now when the congregation had broken up, many of the Jews and devout proselytes followed Paul and Barnabas, who, speaking to them, persuaded them to continue in the grace of God. 44 On the next Sabbath almost the whole city came together to hear the word of God. 45 But when the Jews saw the multitudes, they were filled with envy; and contradicting and blaspheming, they opposed the things spoken by Paul. 46 Then Paul and Barnabas grew bold and said, "It was necessary that the word of God should be spoken to you first; but since you reject it, and judge yourselves unworthy of everlasting life, behold, we turn to the Gentiles. 47 For so the Lord has commanded us: 'I have set you as a light to the Gentiles, that you should be for salvation to the ends of the earth.' " 48 Now when the Gentiles heard this, they were glad and glorified the word of the Lord. And as many as had been appointed to eternal life believed. 49 And the word of the Lord was being spread throughout all the region. 50 But the Jews stirred up the devout and prominent women and the chief men of the city, raised up persecution against Paul and Barnabas, and expelled them from their region. 51 But they shook off the dust from their feet against them, and came to Iconium. 52 And the disciples were filled with joy and with the Holy Spirit.*

INTRODUCTION
A. Acts 13 starts the church in world missions.
B. Antioch becomes the center or hub of activity in the church, where they are first called Christians and where they gave to Jerusalem.
C. Not only does the church have a mission, but each one of us has a call or mission. WE HAVE A MISSION.
D. Let's look at the church motivated by mission, the church mobilized for mission and the church that manifested its mission.

I.   The Church Motivated By Mission
A. The mission was birthed out of worshipping the Lord.
   1. There were in Antioch certain prophets and teachers.
      a. Barnabas, Simeon who was called Niger, Lucius of Cyrene, Manaen who had been brought up by Herod the tetrarch and Saul
      b. Christianity should draw people together and unify them.
   2. They ministered to the Lord and fasted.
      a. They were a worshipping and praying church.
      b. God spoke as they ministered to Him. They had the right priority: PUT GOD FIRST!
      c. We need to gather around Him.
      d. Worship is intimacy with God.
B. The Lord calls Saul and Barnabas to their mission.
   1. Called = in the perfect tense meaning that the two had an inner call which the church recognized by releasing them to the task.
   2. The church's responsibility was to recognize what the Holy Spirit had accomplished in creating the desire and clarifying the direction.
   3. They prayed and laid their hands on them. They sent them away.

APPLICATION
A. We are called by God and indwelt by the Holy Spirit.
B. God prepares us for our mission by everything we go through in our lives.
C. First of all you are called to be with Him. (Mark 3:14)

II. **The Church Mobilized For Mission**
   A. Saul and Barnabas were sent forth - mobilized.
      1. They went to Cyprus. Barnabas was a Levite of Cyprus. (Acts 4:36) He took the gospel to his own people. John Mark went with them.
      2. At Paphos they found Sergius Paulus who was the governor of Cyprus. Many men like Sergius Paulus kept private wizards, fortune tellers, magicians, etc.
         a. Sergius desired to hear the word of God. God has people whom He has placed in our paths who desire to hear the word of God.
         b. Bar-Jesus or Elymas, the sorcerer withstood them. STAND in the spiritual battle. Spiritual conflict is on for the souls of men. He wanted to turn Sergius Paulus away from the faith.
         c. Saul filled with the Holy Spirit, set his eyes on him and said, "O full of all deceit and all fraud, you Son of the devil, you enemy of all righteousness, will you not cease perverting the straight ways of the Lord?"
         d. The hand of the Lord came upon him and smote him with blindness for a season.
         e. Then Sergius Paulus saw what was done and was astonished at the teaching of the Lord. I Cor. 4:20 - *For the kingdom of God is not in word but in power.* He will confirm His word with signs & wonders following!
   B. John Mark is demobilized.
      1. He returned to Jerusalem.
      2. Mark was young. His mother's house was at the center of the church at Jerusalem. Barnabas received him later, but Paul much later. By the grace of God, the quitter becomes the writer of Mark's gospel. Have you failed? God loves to make failures successful!
   C. They are mobilized to the Synagogue.
      1. The law and the prophets are read.
      2. Paul stands up and preaches.
         a. He brought Isreal out of Egypt.
         b. He destroyed nations in the promised land.
         c. He gave them judges 450 years and Samuel the Prophet.
         d. They desired a king – He gave them Saul.
         e. He raised up David, a man after his own heart.
         f. He raised up from the seed of David, Jesus. John the Baptist testified of Him.
         g. Pilate slew Him.
         h. He died and rose again.
      3. The culmination of the message.
         a. v. 38 – Jesus can forgive sins.
         b. v. 39 – all who believe are justified. Justified = dikaio themai - to discern right, accept, acquit. Free or freedom. The cross purchased our Justification and freedom.
         c. v. 40, 41 - unbelief keeps back - He will work a work.

APPLICATION
A. Are we mobilized for our mission?
B. Paul's background was used by God - yours will be too!
C. God loves us and forgives us. Are there any John Marks out there?

III. The Church That Manifested Its Mission
   A. Bar-Jesus and his power were limited against God's power through Paul.
   B. The Jews wanted Paul and Barnabas to preach!
      1. They persuaded them to continue in the grace of God.
      2. They preached the next week.
   C. The manifestation of God caused the manifestation of darkness to be exposed.
      1. The whole city came to hear the word of God.
      2. The Jews were filled with envy and spoke against those things.
      3. Paul and Barnabas were bold and said, "Because you think you are unworthy we go to the Gentiles."
      4. The Jews stirred up the honorable women and chief men of the city. They shook the dust off their feet against them. They were filled with joy and with the Holy Spirit.

APPLICATION
   A. Are you being persecuted for righteousness' sake? Shake the dust off your feet!
   B. Do not judge yourself unworthy. Christ died and rose for you!

THE MISSION CONTINUES

Acts 14 - Now it happened in Iconium that they went together to the synagogue of the Jews, and so spoke that a great multitude both of the Jews and of the Greeks believed. 2 But the unbelieving Jews stirred up the Gentiles and poisoned their minds against the brethren. 3 Therefore they stayed there a long time, speaking boldly in the Lord, who was bearing witness to the word of His grace, granting signs and wonders to be done by their hands. 4 But the multitude of the city was divided: part sided with the Jews, and part with the apostles. 5 And when a violent attempt was made by both the Gentiles and Jews, with their rulers, to abuse and stone them, 6 they became aware of it and fled to Lystra and Derbe, cities of Lycaonia, and to the surrounding region. 7 And they were preaching the gospel there. 8 And in Lystra a certain man without strength in his feet was sitting, a cripple from his mother's womb, who had never walked. 9 This man heard Paul speaking. Paul, observing him intently and seeing that he had faith to be healed, 10 said with a loud voice, "Stand up straight on your feet!" And he leaped and walked. 11 Now when the people saw what Paul had done, they raised their voices, saying in the Lycaonian language, "The gods have come down to us in the likeness of men!" 12 And Barnabas they called Zeus, and Paul, Hermes, because he was the chief speaker. 13 Then the priest of Zeus, whose temple was in front of their city, brought oxen and garlands to the gates, intending to sacrifice with the multitudes. 14 But when the apostles Barnabas and Paul heard this, they tore their clothes and ran in among the multitude, crying out 15 and saying, "Men, why are you doing these things? We also are men with the same nature as you, and preach to you that you should turn from these useless things to the living God, who made the heaven, the earth, the sea, and all things that are in them, 16 who in bygone generations allowed all nations to walk in their own ways. 17 Nevertheless He did not leave Himself without witness, in that He did good, gave us rain from heaven and fruitful seasons, filling our hearts with food and gladness." 18 And with these sayings they could scarcely restrain the multitudes from sacrificing to them. 19 Then Jews from Antioch and Iconium came there; and having persuaded the multitudes, they stoned Paul and dragged him out of the city, supposing him to be dead. 20 However, when the disciples gathered around him, he rose up and went into the city. And the next day he departed with Barnabas to Derbe. 21 And when they had preached the gospel to that city and made many disciples, they returned to Lystra, Iconium, and Antioch, 22 strengthening the souls of the disciples, exhorting them to continue in the faith, and saying, "We must through many tribulations enter the kingdom of God." 23 So when they had appointed elders in every church, and prayed with fasting, they commended them to the Lord in whom they had believed. 24 And after they had passed through Pisidia, they came to Pamphylia. 25 Now when they had preached the word in Perga, they went down to Attalia. 26 From there they sailed to Antioch, where they had been commended to the grace of God for the work which they had completed. 27 Now when they had come and gathered the church together, they reported all that God had done with them, and that He had opened the door of faith to the Gentiles. 28 So they stayed there a long time with the disciples.

INTRODUCTION
A. Christianity involves the supernatural power of God.
B. The regular life of the early Christian was not all excitement and exhilaration there can be mundane times as well.
C. Paul, the Apostle, had one of the most exciting lives on earth but he also faced many hardships.
D. Let's look as evangelizing the lost, exalting the Lord, and establishing the church and how it applies to our lives.

I. **Evangelizing The Lost**
   A. Paul and Barnabas WENT. Jesus commanded us to GO. As we are going, we make disciples, etc. We must reach the lost.
   B. Action! In Iconium they went to the synagogue and spoke to the Jews and the Greeks.
   C. They "so spoke" or so effectively spoke that a multitude believed. Do we "so speak" that people believe and receive Christ?
      1. 1 Corinthians 2:1-5 - *And I, brethren, when I came to you, did not come with excellence of speech or of wisdom declaring to you the testimony of God. For I determined not to know anything among you except Jesus Christ and Him crucified. I was with you in weakness, in fear, and in much trembling. And my speech and my preaching were not with persuasive words of human wisdom, but in demonstration of the Spirit and of power, that your faith should not be in the wisdom of men but in the power of God.*
      2. Mark 16:19-20 - *So then, after the Lord had spoken to them, He was received up into heaven, and sat down at the right hand of God. And they went out and preached everywhere, the Lord working with them and confirming the word through the accompanying signs. Amen.*
   D. The unbelieving Jews stirred up the Gentiles and caused their minds to be turned against the brothers.
   E. They spoke boldly for the Lord. God confirmed the word of His grace. We are to combine a holy boldness, zeal and confidence with the message of God's love.
   F. The Lord wrought signs and wonders by their hands. God uses power evangelism to draw people's attention to Christ and the Gospel. When the church is first being planted there is a great emphasis on the supernatural. Signs follow believers - confirming the word. God desires to use our hands to work miracles.
   G. This caused a multitude of people in the city to be divided. Some of them sided with the Jews and others with the apostles. Both Sides attempted to stone them but the apostles left the area fleeing to Lystra and Derbe while continuing to preach the gospel. Communicators must deal with rejection,discouragement. One rejection can tip the scales against 100 affirmations.
   H. At Lystra there was a man without strength in his feet, crippled since birth heard Paul speak. Paul perceived that the man had faith to be healed and commanded him to, "Stand up straight on your feet!" The man leaped and walked. Be sensitive to the Holy Spirit. Do not grieve Him.

APPLICATION
   A. Are we evangelizing the lost? Speak in His power. We are baptized in the Holy Spirit to be witnesses.
   B. Speak boldly the word of His grace! Expect opposition. We can expect the kingdom of darkness to resist.
   C. We can expect God to advance His kingdom with greater might.

II. **Exalting The Lord**
   A. This is positive. Exalt Him! Most of the exalting in this passage was misdirected.
   B. After the miracle they began to worship Paul and Barnabas. According to an ancient legend, Hermes and Zeus had descended into that region a long time ago. The people said now the gods had come to earth. Barnabas was called Zeus and Paul Hermes because he was the chief speaker.
      1. We are not gods.
      2. We are men.
   C. They brought sacrifices to worship, but Paul and Barnabas tore their clothes. They said we are men of like passions!
      1. John 3:30 - *He must increase, but I must decrease.*
      2. Men's hearts tend toward idolatry. Power, sex, money, position, fame, beauty and pleasure to name a few.
      3. There are idols in the church. Our heroes, our teachings, etc...there can be many things substituted for the true worship of God.

4. Be careful not to put men and women of God on a pedestal. Don't praise and position them where only God should be. Don't make yourself God and appropriate to yourself what is God's prerogative. He will not share His glory with another!
5. Herod died in Acts 12 because he tried to steal the glory that was due God alone.
D. Paul and Barnabas would not be exalted and worshiped!
   1. They preached for them to turn from their vanities unto the living God. REPENT!
   2. God made everything. He left a witness in nature. The multitudes were made aware of their position before God.
   3. They refused to accept the glory and the worship of men. The Jews from Antioch and Iconium persuaded the multitudes to stone Paul and leave him for dead.

APPLICATION
A. Exalt the Lord!
B. Decrease, let Him increase!
C. Read I Peter 5:5-11 - that tells it all!

III. Establishing The Church
A. God raised Paul from the dead. God delivers in many ways. As the disciples stood around him he arose and went to Derbe. Stand around and pray.
B. Sometimes there is a danger in being popular.
C. The excitement died down a bit. They went back to Lystra, Iconium and Antioch.
D. Paul went back to establish the church. He went back to where he had been stoned.
E. He exhorted them to continue in the faith. He had proclaimed the blood of Jesus, the resurrection, and the message of forgiveness,but they needed to be taught the whole counsel of God.
F. He exhorted them to see that through much tribulation we enter into the kingdom of God. It will cost us something to see God's kingdom established.
G. Matthew 11:12 - *And from the days of John the Baptist until now the kingdom of heaven suffers violence, and the violent take it by force.*
H. The establishment of the local churches involved:
   1. Confirmation - reestablishment or further support.
   2. Exhortation - to instruct and encourage them in the faith to live for God in this dark world.
   3. Organization - elders in every church by prayer and fasting. He commended the elders to the Lord in whom they believed.
I. They went back to Antioch and gave testimony of what God had done.

APPLICATION: God wants to establish us. I exhort and confirm. Let us pray for the elders.

PROBLEMS

Acts 15 - And certain men came down from Judea and taught the brethren, "Unless you are circumcised according to the custom of Moses, you cannot be saved." 2 Therefore, when Paul and Barnabas had no small dissension and dispute with them, they determined that Paul and Barnabas and certain others of them should go up to Jerusalem, to the apostles and elders, about this question. 3 So, being sent on their way by the church, they passed through Phoenicia and Samaria, describing the conversion of the Gentiles; and they caused great joy to all the brethren. 4 And when they had come to Jerusalem, they were received by the church and the apostles and the elders; and they reported all things that God had done with them. 5 But some of the sect of the Pharisees who believed rose up, saying, "It is necessary to circumcise them, and to command them to keep the law of Moses." 6 Now the apostles and elders came together to consider this matter. 7 And when there had been much dispute, Peter rose up and said to them: "Men and brethren, you know that a good while ago God chose among us, that by my mouth the Gentiles should hear the word of the gospel and believe. 8 So God, who knows the heart, acknowledged them by giving them the Holy Spirit, just as He did to us, 9 and made no distinction between us and them, purifying their hearts by faith. 10 Now therefore, why do you test God by putting a yoke on the neck of the disciples which neither our fathers nor we were able to bear? 11 But we believe that through the grace of the Lord Jesus Christ we shall be saved in the same manner as they." 12 Then all the multitude kept silent and listened to Barnabas and Paul declaring how many miracles and wonders God had worked through them among the Gentiles. 13 And after they had become silent, James answered, saying, "Men and brethren, listen to me: 14 Simon has declared how God at the first visited the Gentiles to take out of them a people for His name. 15 And with this the words of the prophets agree, just as it is written: 16 'After this I will return and will rebuild the tabernacle of David, which has fallen down; I will rebuild its ruins, and I will set it up; 17 So that the rest of mankind may seek the Lord, Even all the Gentiles who are called by My name, Says the Lord who does all these things.' 18 "Known to God from eternity are all His works. 19 Therefore I judge that we should not trouble those from among the Gentiles who are turning to God, 20 but that we write to them to abstain from things polluted by idols, from sexual immorality, from things strangled, and from blood. 21 For Moses has had throughout many generations those who preach him in every city, being read in the synagogues every Sabbath." 22 Then it pleased the apostles and elders, with the whole church, to send chosen men of their own company to Antioch with Paul and Barnabas, namely, Judas who was also named Barsabas, and Silas, leading men among the brethren. 23 They wrote this letter by them: the apostles, the elders, and the brethren, To the brethren who are of the Gentiles in Antioch, Syria, and Cilicia: Greetings. 24 Since we have heard that some who went out from us have troubled you with words, unsettling your souls, saying, "You must be circumcised and keep the law"—to whom we gave no such commandment— 25 it seemed good to us, being assembled with one accord, to send chosen men to you with our beloved Barnabas and Paul, 26 men who have risked their lives for the name of our Lord Jesus Christ. 27 We have therefore sent Judas and Silas, who will also report the same things by word of mouth. 28 For it seemed good to the Holy Spirit, and to us, to lay upon you no greater burden than these necessary things: 29 that you abstain from things offered to idols, from blood, from things strangled, and from sexual immorality. If you keep yourselves from these, you will do well. Farewell. 30 So when they were sent off, they came to Antioch; and when they had gathered the multitude together, they delivered the letter. 31 When they had read it, they rejoiced over its encouragement. 32 Now Judas and Silas, themselves being prophets also, exhorted and strengthened the brethren with many words. 33 And after they had stayed there for a time, they were sent back with greetings from the brethren to the apostles. 34 However, it seemed good to Silas to remain there. 35 Paul and Barnabas also remained in Antioch, teaching and preaching the word of the Lord, with many others also. 36 Then after some days Paul said to Barnabas, "Let us now go back and *visit our brethren in every city where we have preached the word of the Lord, and see how they are doing." 37 Now Barnabas was determined to take with them John called Mark. 38 But Paul insisted that they should not take with them the one who had departed from them in Pamphylia, and had not gone with them to the work. 39 Then the contention became so sharp that they parted from one another. And so Barnabas took Mark and sailed to Cyprus; 40 but Paul chose Silas and departed, being commended by the brethren to the grace of God. 41 And he went through Syria and Cilicia, strengthening the churches.*

INTRODUCTION

A. At the end of chapter 14 Paul and Barnabas are back at home base of Antioch in Syria. On their first missionary journey they had planted four churches in Galatia (Antioch of Pisidia, Iconium, Lystra and Derbe).

B. V1 - The time is A.D. 48. The first Gentile churches had been planted in Antioch in AD 45.

C. In this part of Acts the message of exclusion was rearing its ugly head. We need to be Christ-centered.

D. Every person has a need for meaning, purpose, and the feeling of being loved and accepted.

E. Let's see what we can learn from Acts 15.

I. Differences And Difficulties

A. Men came from Judea and said you could not be saved unless you were circumcised after the manner of Moses.

   1. Some Jews were willing that the Gentiles should come into the church, but on the condition they become Jews.

   2. Paul and Barnabas disagreed with them. This caused dissension and disputes.

B. They went to Jerusalem to seek counsel.

   1. Proverbs 15:22 - *Without counsel, plans go awry, but in the multitude of counselors they are established.*

   2. Proverbs 11:14 - *Where there is no counsel, the people fall; but in the multitude of counselors there is safety.*

   3. They went through Phoenicia and Samaria and declared that the Gentiles had been converted. This filled the people with joy.

APPLICATION

   1. Do we seek godly counsel?

   2. Psalm 1

   3. We have differences and difficulties, but God can use these to draw us closer together.

II. Dialogue And Discussion

A. They declared what God had done to the elders and apostles.

   1. In the midst of this a certain sect of the Pharisees rose up saying it was needful for them to be circumcised according to the law of Moses.

      a. It was not the physical act of circumcision alone, but the instruction in the law and the pledge to keep it, which preceded the ritual they had in mind.

      b. Galatians 3:24-25 - *Therefore the law was our tutor to bring us to Christ, that we might be justified by faith. But after faith has come, we are no longer under a tutor.*

      c. Ephesians 2:8-10 - *For by grace you have been saved through faith, and that not of yourselves; it is the gift of God, not of works, lest anyone should boast. For we are His workmanship, created in Christ Jesus for good works, which God prepared beforehand that we should walk in them.*

      d. "The paradox of Christianity is that the way to victory is surrender. And the way to power is through admitting one's own helplessness."[3] - William Barclay

      e. We are saved by grace and we walk by grace.

B. The apostles and elders considered the matter.
1. Peter spoke about how God used him.
    a. History - Cornelius and the Gentiles, salvation and baptism with the Holy Spirit.
    b. Cohesion - God placed no difference between us, purifying their hearts by faith. Don't tempt God. "...neither our fathers nor we were able to bear? But we believe that through the grace of the Lord Jesus Christ we shall be saved in the same manner as they."
2. Barnabas and Paul declared the miracles that God had done among the Gentiles through them.
3. James heard and answered them.
    a. He told them what Peter said. He appeared to be the leader.
    b. He told them what the prophets had written.
        i. "After this I will return and will rebuild the tabernacle of David, which has fallen down; I will rebuild its ruins, and I will set it up; so that the rest of mankind may seek the Lord, even all the Gentiles who are called by My name, says the Lord who does all these things'."
        ii. James makes a decision not to trouble the Gentiles but to let them know that they should abstain from the pollution of idols, sexual immorality, things that had been strangled and blood.

APPLICATION: With problems we need dialogue, discussion and leadership. God will restore and build the tabernacle of David.

III. Decision And Direction: The church decides and directs
A. They acted with courtesy and efficiency. The letter was entrusted to Judas and Silas who went with Paul and Barnabas.
B. It seemed good to them and the Holy Spirit to lay no great burden than what was necessary.
C. Decision determines direction. The lesson of Acceptance: Will I accept people as God accepts people?
D. Many people experience rejection; people putting things on them. Jesus lifts off burdens.
E. They went and affirmed the people. They loved and helped them.
F. There was a contention about Mark between Paul and Barnabas. Thank God for Barnabas.

APPLICATION: God wants us to make decisions and it will help our direction. Great men and women make great decisions.

EXPECTING THE UNEXPECTED

Acts 16 - *Then he came to Derbe and Lystra. And behold, a certain disciple was there, named Timothy, the son of a certain Jewish woman who believed, but his father was Greek. 2 He was well spoken of by the brethren who were at Lystra and Iconium. 3 Paul wanted to have him go on with him. And he took him and circumcised him because of the Jews who were in that region, for they all knew that his father was Greek. 4 And as they went through the cities, they delivered to them the decrees to keep, which were determined by the apostles and elders at Jerusalem. 5 So the churches were strengthened in the faith, and increased in number daily. 6 Now when they had gone through Phrygia and the region of Galatia, they were forbidden by the Holy Spirit to preach the word in Asia. 7 After they had come to Mysia, they tried to go into Bithynia, but the Spirit did not permit them. 8 So passing by Mysia, they came down to Troas. 9 And a vision appeared to Paul in the night. A man of Macedonia stood and pleaded with him, saying, "Come over to Macedonia and help us." 10 Now after he had seen the vision, immediately we sought to go to Macedonia, concluding that the Lord had called us to preach the gospel to them. 11 Therefore, sailing from Troas, we ran a straight course to Samothrace, and the next day came to Neapolis, 12 and from there to Philippi, which is the foremost city of that part of Macedonia, a colony. And we were staying in that city for some days. 13 And on the Sabbath day we went out of the city to the riverside, where prayer was customarily made; and we sat down and spoke to the women who met there. 14 Now a certain woman named Lydia heard us. She was a seller of purple from the city of Thyatira, who worshiped God. The Lord opened her heart to heed the things spoken by Paul. 15 And when she and her household were baptized, she begged us, saying, "If you have judged me to be faithful to the Lord, come to my house and stay." So she persuaded us. 16 Now it happened, as we went to prayer, that a certain slave girl possessed with a spirit of divination met us, who brought her masters much profit by fortune-telling. 17 This girl followed Paul and us, and cried out, saying, "These men are the servants of the Most High God, who proclaim to us the way of salvation." 18 And this she did for many days. But Paul, greatly annoyed, turned and said to the spirit, "I command you in the name of Jesus Christ to come out of her." And he came out that very hour. 19 But when her masters saw that their hope of profit was gone, they seized Paul and Silas and dragged them into the marketplace to the authorities. 20 And they brought them to the magistrates, and said, "These men, being Jews, exceedingly trouble our city; 21 and they teach customs which are not lawful for us, being Romans, to receive or observe." 22 Then the multitude rose up together against them; and the magistrates tore off their clothes and commanded them to be beaten with rods. 23 And when they had laid many stripes on them, they threw them into prison, commanding the jailer to keep them securely. 24 Having received such a charge, he put them into the inner prison and fastened their feet in the stocks. 25 But at midnight Paul and Silas were praying and singing hymns to God, and the prisoners were listening to them. 26 Suddenly there was a great earthquake, so that the foundations of the prison were shaken; and immediately all the doors were opened and everyone's chains were loosed. 27 And the keeper of the prison, awaking from sleep and seeing the prison doors open, supposing the prisoners had fled, drew his sword and was about to kill himself. 28 But Paul called with a loud voice, saying, "Do yourself no harm, for we are all here." 29 Then he called for a light, ran in, and fell down trembling before Paul and Silas. 30 And he brought them out and said, "Sirs, what must I do to be saved?" 31 So they said, "Believe on the Lord Jesus Christ, and you will be saved, you and your household." 32 Then they spoke the word of the Lord to him and to all who were in his house. 33 And he took them the same hour of the night and washed their stripes. And immediately he and all his family were baptized. 34 Now when he had brought them into his house, he set food before them; and he rejoiced, having believed in God with all his household. 35 And when it was day, the magistrates sent the officers, saying, "Let those men go." 36 So the keeper of the prison reported these words to Paul, saying, "The magistrates have sent to let you go. Now therefore depart, and go in peace." 37 But Paul said to them, "They have beaten us openly, uncondemned Romans, and have thrown us into prison. And now do they put us out secretly? No indeed! Let them come themselves and get us out." 38 And the officers told these words to the magistrates, and they were afraid when they heard that they were Romans. 39 Then they came and pleaded with them and brought them out, and asked them to depart from the city. 40 So they went out of the prison and entered the house of Lydia; and when they had seen the brethren, they encouraged them and departed.*

INTRODUCTION
A. We can be an optimist or a pessimist.
B. We need to look at things in a right perspective.
C. We can out-plan God. We must be open to what He wants.
D. Expect the unexpected. Let's look at the direction of God's Spirit, the difficulties of God's servant, and the deliverance of God's saints and how it applies to us.

I. The Direction Of God's Spirit
A. Paul went to Lystra. He was stoned there. He refused worship there. God gave Timothy to Paul in Lystra in the midst of hardtimes. Paul had team ministry.
B. Timothy was circumcised.
   1. "This was a case of expedience, in order for the fulfillment of the ministry." - G. Campbell Morgan.
   2. Paul knew that the Jews would criticize.
   3. "The reason for circumcision was not theological; it was missiological." - C. Peter Wagner. They advanced the kingdom - churches established in the faith and increased in number daily.
C. Paul had planned to go to key cities. God did not allow him to go to Asia or Bithynia. In Galatians it says his infirmity stopped him from going.
   1. God opens doors and closes doors. Forbidden -koluthentes - to hinder, closed door.
   2. I Corinthians 16:9 - *For a great and effective door has opened to me, and there are many adversaries." Sometimes the enemy tries to hinder us.* I Thessalonians 2:18 - *Therefore we wanted to come to you—even I, Paul, time and again - but Satan hindered us.*
   3. The Holy Spirit guides by the Word, His still small voice, circumstances, difficult things, disappointing things, etc. Have a right attitude. The Holy Spirit leads men and women who look, watch, wait and follow. God's direction will bring great challenge. His no may be a better yes possibility.
   4. Paul comes to Troas.

APPLICATION:
A. God will direct us.
B. Sometimes an open door; sometimes a closed door. Look and watch, wait and follow. Be sensitive. Pray and read the Word of God.
C. Let God give you His vision.
D. Timothy signed up for warfare.
   1. I Timothy 1:18 - *This charge I commit to you, son Timothy, according to the prophecies previously made concerning you, that by them you may wage the good warfare...*
   2. II Timothy 2:3-4 - *You therefore must endure hardship as a good soldier of Jesus Christ. No one engaged in warfare entangles himself with the affairs of this life, that he may please him who enlisted him as a soldier.*
   3. I Timothy 6:12 - *Fight the good fight of faith, lay hold on eternal life, to which you were also called and have confessed the good confession in the presence of many witnesses.*

II. The Difficulties Of God's Servants
A. Satanic Opposition
   1. They went with a 'straight course' - out ahead of the wind. Sometimes the wind is at our back and others times it is a contrary wind in our face. They came to Philippi.

2. Lydia and her family are saved and baptized. The Lord "opened her heart." Does the Lord need to open your heart?
3. A woman with a spirit of divination was bringing a satanic message.
    a. Do not let evil give verification to who you are.
    b. Do not be surprised at demonic opposition.
    c. Do enter into spiritual warfare.
    d. Paul was grieved. He commanded the spirit to come out of her in the Name of Jesus Christ.
    e. We are in CHRIST. We are VICTORS! Do not believe the enemy's lies!
B. Carnal Opposition
1. Men get upset over losing money and power.
2. They have Paul and Silas arrested and whipped.

APPLICATION:
1. Expect opposition. Expect God to help.
2. Has God led you to help when you were in the midst of trouble?
3. Join the Paul and Silas club. We are advancing the kingdom. Opposition develops when God is just about to do something with you.

III. THE DELIVERANCE OF GOD'S SAINTS.
A. Paul and Silas are placed in the inner prison in stocks. They have scars on their backs.
B. Philippians 1:29-30 - *For to you it has been granted on behalf of Christ, not only to believe in Him, but also to suffer for His sake, having the same conflict which you saw in me and now hear is in me.*
C. Adversity, disappointment, and trouble does not mean God has forsaken us. 'Many are the afflictions of the righteous, but the Lord delivers us out of them all.'
D. In the midnight hour they prayed and sang praises.
1. As they praised they did spiritual battle.
2. An earthquake shook the foundations of the prison and the doors were opened. Praise and prayer breaks us out of prisons and others as well.
E. The Philippian jailor is ready to kill himself, but Paul tells him, 'But Paul called with a loud voice, saying, "Do yourself no harm, for we are all here." Then he called for a light, ran in, and fell down trembling before Paul and Silas. And he brought them out and said, "Sirs, what must I do to be saved?" So they said, "Believe on the Lord Jesus Christ, and you will be saved, you and your household."
1. He is saved and baptized.
2. He ministers to them.
3. He opens his house to them.
F. The magistrate sent officers to let them go. Paul was a Roman citizen and these men had broken the law by beating them.

APPLICATION:
A. God will deliver us! You are special to God.
B. God delivers His saints. You are a saint.
C. Others will be delivered too.

BE A LIGHT IN THE DARKNESS

Acts 17 - *1 Now when they had passed through Amphipolis and Apollonia, they came to Thessalonica, where there was a synagogue of the Jews. 2 Then Paul, as his custom was, went in to them, and for three Sabbaths reasoned with them from the Scriptures, 3 explaining and demonstrating that the Christ had to suffer and rise again from the dead, and saying, "This Jesus whom I preach to you is the Christ." 4 And some of them were persuaded; and a great multitude of the devout Greeks, and not a few of the leading women, joined Paul and Silas. 5 But the Jews who were not persuaded, becoming envious, took some of the evil men from the marketplace, and gathering a mob, set all the city in an uproar and attacked the house of Jason, and sought to bring them out to the people. 6 But when they did not find them, they dragged Jason and some brethren to the rulers of the city, crying out, "These who have turned the world upside down have come here too. 7 Jason has harbored them, and these are all acting contrary to the decrees of Caesar, saying there is another king—Jesus." 8 And they troubled the crowd and the rulers of the city when they heard these things. 9 So when they had taken security from Jason and the rest, they let them go. 10 Then the brethren immediately sent Paul and Silas away by night to Berea. When they arrived, they went into the synagogue of the Jews. 11 These were more fair-minded than those in Thessalonica, in that they received the word with all readiness, and searched the Scriptures daily to find out whether these things were so. 12 Therefore many of them believed, and also not a few of the Greeks, prominent women as well as men. 13 But when the Jews from Thessalonica learned that the word of God was preached by Paul at Berea, they came there also and stirred up the crowds. 14 Then immediately the brethren sent Paul away, to go to the sea; but both Silas and Timothy remained there. 15 So those who conducted Paul brought him to Athens; and receiving a command for Silas and Timothy to come to him with all speed, they departed. 16 Now while Paul waited for them at Athens, his spirit was provoked within him when he saw that the city was given over to idols. 17 Therefore he reasoned in the synagogue with the Jews and with the Gentile worshipers, and in the marketplace daily with those who happened to be there. 18 Then certain Epicurean and Stoic philosophers encountered him. And some said, "What does this babbler want to say?" Others said, "He seems to be a proclaimer of foreign gods," because he preached to them Jesus and the resurrection. 19 And they took him and brought him to the Areopagus, saying, "May we know what this new doctrine is of which you speak? 20 For you are bringing some strange things to our ears. Therefore we want to know what these things mean." 21 For all the Athenians and the foreigners who were there spent their time in nothing else but either to tell or to hear some new thing. 22 Then Paul stood in the midst of the Areopagus and said, "Men of Athens, I perceive that in all things you are very religious; 23 for as I was passing through and considering the objects of your worship, I even found an altar with this inscription: Therefore, the One whom you worship without knowing, Him I proclaim to you: 24 God, who made the world and everything in it, since He is Lord of heaven and earth, does not dwell in temples made with hands. 25 Nor is He worshiped with men's hands, as though He needed anything, since He gives to all life, breath, and all things. 26 And He has made from one blood every nation of men to dwell on all the face of the earth, and has determined their preappointed times and the boundaries of their dwellings, 27 so that they should seek the Lord, in the hope that they might grope for Him and find Him, though He is not far from each one of us; 28 for in Him we live and move and have our being, as also some of your own poets have said, 'For we are also His offspring.' 29 Therefore, since we are the offspring of God, we ought not to think that the Divine Nature is like gold or silver or stone, something shaped by art and man's devising. 30 Truly, these times of ignorance God overlooked, but now commands all men everywhere to repent, 31 because He has appointed a day on which He will judge the world in righteousness by the Man whom He has ordained. He has given assurance of this to all by raising Him from the dead." 32 And when they heard of the resurrection of the dead, some mocked, while others said, "We will hear you again on this matter." 33 So Paul departed from among them. 34 However, some men joined him and believed, among them Dionysius the Areopagite, a woman named Damaris, and others with them.*

INTRODUCTION

A. The Lord Jesus didn't say, "Let your light so twinkle....but let it 'shine!'".

B. Matthew 5:14-16 - *You are the light of the world. A city that is set on a hill cannot be hidden. Nor do they light a lamp and put it under a basket, but on a lampstand, and it gives light to all who are in the house. Let your light so shine before men, that they may see your good works and glorify your Father in heaven.*

C. Harvest. I Corinthians 3:6, Paul said, "I planted, Apollos watered, but God gave the increase."

D. We live in a dark age. We have been delivered from the kingdom of darkness and translated into the kingdom of light or of His dear Son.

E. Let's look at Paul's motive, method and message of being a light in the darkness.

I. Paul's Motive For Being A Light

A. He had a motive of love that drove him.
   1. Thessalonica was a key city for the gospel to spread from east to west. It was the capital of Macedonia; passing through Amphipolis, Apollonia and then ending at Thessalonica, covering a distance of over 100 miles.
   2. II Corinthians 5:14 - *For the love of Christ compels us, because we judge thus: that if One died for all, then all died.*
   3. Acts 26:16-18 - *But rise and stand on your feet; for I have appeared to you for this purpose, to make you a minister and a witness both of the things which you have seen and of the things which I will yet reveal to you. I will deliver you from the Jewish people, as well as from the Gentiles, to whom I now send you, to open their eyes, in order to turn them from darkness to light, and from the power of Satan to God, that they may receive forgiveness of sins and an inheritance among those who are sanctified by faith in Me.*

B. He had a motive to see every man acknowledge King Jesus.
   1. He preached Jesus is the Christ and alleged that Christ had to suffer and rise from the dead.
   2. A great multitude of devout Greeks and women believed and joined Paul and Silas.
   3. Some did not believe Paul. The Jews were moved with envy and gathered a mob of evil men. They set all the city in an uproar and attacked the house of Jason.
   4. When they did not find Paul they took Jason and some of the brothers crying, "These who have turned the world upside down have come here too."
      a. One child remarked that the New Testament ended with revolutions. They turned the world upside down and caused a "revolution".
      b. When we shine as light in the darkness....we stir up the darkness.
   5. They said they did contrary to the decrees of Caeser saying there is another King-Jesus! When they had taken security from Jason and the rest, they let them go.

APPLICATION:

1. Are you motivated by love to reach the lost?
2. Are you motivated to proclaim Jesus until they join the kingdom?
3. Let's turn the world upside down!
4. I Thessalonians 1:5 - *For our gospel did not come to you in word only, but also in power, and in the Holy Spirit, and in much assurance, as you know what kind of men we were among you for your sake.*

II. Paul's Method For Being A Light.

A. The method of the synagogue.
   1. They had sent Paul and Silas away and went to the synagogue of the Jews. When David Livingstone was asked where he was prepared to go, he answered, "I am prepared to go anywhere, so long as it is forward". Paul was being persecuted again, but would not turn. People then were seeking God. Berea was 60 miles west of Thessolonica.

    2. Paul set the Bereans searching the scriptures. They were more noble than the Thessalonians in that they received the word with readiness of mind. Do we have a readiness of mind?

    3. They searched the scriptures daily. The Jews of Thessalonica learned what Paul was doing. They stirred the people up against Paul. They had to send Paul away.

  B. The method of teamwork.

    1. Later, Timothy and Silas joined Paul. Luke 10 says they were sent out in teams of two. We need teamwork.

    2. Who has God teamed you up with?

APPLICATION:

1. Start where people are at! Expect darkness to oppose you.
2. Ask God for a partner or partners.
3. Ecclesiastes 4:9-12 - *Two are better then one, because they have a good reward for their labor. For if they fall, one will lift of his companion. But woe to him who is alone when he falls, for he has no one to help him up. Again, if two lie down together, they will keep warm; But how can one be warm alone? Though one may be over powered by another, two can withstand him. And a threefold cord is not quickly broken.*

III. Paul's Message For Being A Light

  A. A message of the heart.

    1. While Paul waited in Athens he was stirred in the spirit, when he saw the city had given into idolatry. Athens is named after Athena - the goddess of wisdom, fine and skilled arts. She is on the official seal of the government of California.

      a. It reminds me of Kathmandu Nepal.

      b. It was a city of many gods.

      c. Do you get stirred? Are you fired up for God? If not, pray Ezekiel 36:25-28 - *Then I will sprinkle clean water on you, and you shall be clean; I will cleanse you from all your filthiness and from all your idols. I will give you a new heart and put a New spirit within you; I will take the heart of stone out of your flesh and give you a heart of flesh. I will put My Spirit within you and cause you to walk in My statutes, and you will keep My judgments and do them. Then you shall dwell in the land that I gave to your fathers; you shall be My people, and I will be your God.*

  B. A message of reason.

    1. He reasoned in the synagogue with the Jews and the Gentile worshipers. He then reasoned in the marketplace. Are you reasoning in the marketplace?

    2. He dwelt with the Epicureans and the Stoics.

      a. Epicureans believed:

        i. Everything happened by chance.

        ii. That death was the end of all.

        iii. That the gods were remote from the world and did not care at all.

        iv. That pleasure was the chief end of man.

      b. Stoics believed:

        i. Everything was God.

        ii. Everything that happened was the will of God.

        iii. That every so often the world disintegrated and started over again.

      c. They said, "What does this 'blabbler' want to Say". Blabbler is a seed picker. They discerned Paul's intelligence. The gospel will bring disputing as it is reasoned. These people were spending their time in nothing else. How are you spending your time?

  C. A message of Jesus Christ.

    1. Paul stood in the midst of Mar's Hill. He perceived they were superstitious. He found an altar to an unknown god. The altar was in case they had over looked a god.

2. Paul declared who the unknown God is!
   a. God is the creator - He made all things.
   b. God has guided history - His story.
   c. God made man to long after Him.
   d. The day of judgment is coming! We will stand. He has appointed a day.
   e. The proof of the pre-eminence of Christ is the resurrection.
3. The key of the message is repent! Metaneo - change your mind, think over again, reconsider its position, get away from false concepts. The result is some mock, some postponed and some received.
4. Dionysius the Areopagite was saved. He was part of the supreme court of the Areopagus. A woman named Damaris was also saved.

APPLICATION:
A. Preach Christ and repentance.
B. It's a message to preach, a message to live.
C. Let your light shine in the darkness.
D. Worship the invisible God, not the visible idols.

BOOK OF ACTS SERIES | LESSON 21
ENCOURAGING GOD'S LABORERS

Acts 18:1-23 - 1 After these things Paul departed from Athens and went to Corinth. 2 And he found a certain Jew named Aquila, born in Pontus, who had recently come from Italy with his wife Priscilla (because Claudius had commanded all the Jews to depart from Rome); and he came to them. 3 So, because he was of the same trade, he stayed with them and worked; for by occupation they were tentmakers. 4 And he reasoned in the synagogue every Sabbath, and persuaded both Jews and Greeks. 5 When Silas and Timothy had come from Macedonia, Paul was compelled by the Spirit, and testified to the Jews that Jesus is the Christ. 6 But when they opposed him and blasphemed, he shook his garments and said to them, "Your blood be upon your own heads; I am clean. From now on I will go to the Gentiles." 7 And he departed from there and entered the house of a certain man named Justus, one who worshiped God, whose house was next door to the synagogue. 8 Then Crispus, the ruler of the synagogue, believed on the Lord with all his household. And many of the Corinthians, hearing, believed and were baptized. 9 Now the Lord spoke to Paul in the night by a vision, "Do not be afraid, but speak, and do not keep silent; 10 for I am with you, and no one will attack you to hurt you; for I have many people in this city." 11 And he continued there a year and six months, teaching the word of God among them. 12 When Gallio was proconsul of Achaia, the Jews with one accord rose up against Paul and brought him to the judgment seat, 13 saying, "This fellow persuades men to worship God contrary to the law." 14 And when Paul was about to open his mouth, Gallio said to the Jews, "If it were a matter of wrongdoing or wicked crimes, O Jews, there would be reason why I should bear with you. 15 But if it is a question of words and names and your own law, look to it yourselves; for I do not want to be a judge of such matters." 16 And he drove them from the judgment seat. 17 Then all the Greeks took Sosthenes, the ruler of the synagogue, and beat him before the judgment seat. But Gallio took no notice of these things. 18 So Paul still remained a good while. Then he took leave of the brethren and sailed for Syria, and Priscilla and Aquila were with him. He had his hair cut off at Cenchrea, for he had taken a vow. 19 And he came to Ephesus, and left them there; but he himself entered the synagogue and reasoned with the Jews. 20 When they asked him to stay a longer time with them, he did not consent, 21 but took leave of them, saying, "I must by all means keep this coming feast in Jerusalem; but I will return again to you, God willing." And he sailed from Ephesus. 22 And when he had landed at Caesarea, and [g]gone up and greeted the church, he went down to Antioch. 23 After he had spent some time there, he departed and went over the region of Galatia and Phrygia [h]in order, strengthening all the disciples.

INTRODUCTION
    A. Encourage:
        1. To inspire with courage or hope
        2. To support or foster
    B. What brings out the best in people is encouragement.
    C. Let's look at how God encouraged one of His laborers, Paul, and how we can learn from it.

I. The Need For God's Laborers To Be Encouraged
    A. Paul was discouraged.
        1. 'After these things' - at Mars Hill he had been mocked and dealt with the philosophers.
        2. He made a 50-mile journey from Athens to Corinth. Paul must have been greatly discouraged.
        3. *I Corinthians 2:1-5 - And I, brethren, when I came to you, did not come with excellence of speech or with wisdom declaring to you the testimony of God. For I determined not to know anything among you except Jesus Christ and Him crucified. I was with you in weakness, in fear, and in much trembling. And my speech and my preaching were not with persuasive words of human wisdom, but in demonstration of the Spirit and of power, that your faith should not be in the*

wisdom of men but in the power of God. He had probably taken a beating from the philosophers. He was not only discouraged, but determined.

   B. We get discouraged.
      1. Have you ever been discouraged as God's laborer? The bold apostle was a candidate for discouragement. The negative attitudes of people, sin suffering in the world, exhaustion from hard work and so on.
      2. Sometimes we are most open to discouragement after great victories. Elijah.
      3. Proverbs 13:12 - *Hope deferred makes the heart sick, But when the desire comes, it is a tree of life.*

APPLICATION:
   A. God understands you when you are discouraged.
   B. He understands when the road gets rough.
   C. He delights to encourage His people.
   D. Psalm 73

II. The Source Of God's Laborers To Be Encouraged
   A. God's method with Paul
      1. God gave Paul new friends or friendships. Paul met Aquila and Priscilla. It was a marketplace relationship. The Lord seldom solves the problem of discouragement without using His people to remind us that we are loved through them. Sometimes fellowship is deepened more when we honestly confess our need and frustration. They Had a common interest. He was of the same craft - tent making. Silas and Timothy came and Paul was pressed.
          a. Hebrews 10:24-25 - *And let us consider one an other in order to stir up love and good works, not forsaking the assembling of ourselves together, as is the manner of some, but exhorting one another, and so much the more as you see the Day approaching.*
          b. Proverbs 27:17 - *As iron sharpens iron; so a man sharpens the countenance of his friend.*
      2. Paul testified to the Jews that Jesus was the Christ. They opposed themselves and blasphemed. So Paul said, "Your blood be upon your own heads; I am clean: from henceforth I will go the Gentiles." Paul was rejected again.
          a. He departed and entered Justus' house next to the synagogue. Then Crispus, the ruler of the synagogue believed and many Corinthians believed and were baptized.
          b. God's method was not only to bring relationships to Paul, but to visit him. God spoke by night in a vision. He said, "Be not afraid, but speak, and hold not your peace. For I am with you, and no man shall hurt you: For I have much people in this city."
              i. He had developed the I-even-I-am-left among the faithful syndrom.
             ii. I am with you. Do not be afraid. Take courage.
            iii. Paul needed his vision rekindled.
           iv. You are not alone. There are many people I have in this city, Corinth. Corinth was dominated by the Temple of Aphrodite. They had one thousand temple prostitutes. It was a city full of immorality. "Everything which he denounced within the church was a reflection of the corruption of the city." - G. Campbell Morgan.
            v. Paul continued teaching the Word of God there for a year and a half.
   B. God's method with us
      1. Friends. Develop friendships. Look to friends to help. God encourages through others. Common interests or crafts will help develop friendships.
      2. Don't forsake the assembling together.
      3. God will give new vision or rekindle an old vision.
      4. You are not alone. God has many people in Everett. He has many people in Snohomish County. (Corinth).

APPLICATION:
  A. Be encouraged, God's laborer. He will bring people your way. Do your part.
  B. He will give fresh vision and strength. Remember your original call. Take one step at a time.

III. The Surprises For God's Laborers To Be Encouraged
  A. Divine intervention for Paul
    1. The Jews made insurrection against Paul and brought him before the judgment seat.
    2. Gallio said he would not judge according to their laws. God spared Paul. God surprises us with His divine intervention.
    3. Then they took Sosthenes, the chief ruler of the synagogue and beat him.
    4. Paul travels on to Antioch through Ephesus, Caesarea and Jerusalem. He shaved his head in Cenchrea for the vow he made expressing his gratitude and recommitment to God's purpose and plan.
    5. He went all over Galatia and Phyrgia in order, strengthening the brethren.
  B. Divine intervention for us
    1. God protects us. When we are attacked, He can work through people and situations.
    2. Isaiah 54:17 - *No weapon formed against you shall prosper, and every tongue which rises against you in judgment you shall condemn. This is the heritage of the servants of the Lord, and their righteousness is from Me, says the Lord.*
    3. We will be able to strengthen others.

APPLICATION:
  A. God wants to encourage you through more surprises. Look for them. Expect them.
  B. I miss signs on the freeway if I do not look for them.

TAKING A CITY WITH GOD

Acts 18:24 - Acts 19:38 - *24 Now a certain Jew named Apollos, born at Alexandria, an eloquent man and mighty in the Scriptures, came to Ephesus. 25 This man had been instructed in the way of the Lord; and being fervent in spirit, he spoke and taught accurately the things of the Lord, though he knew only the baptism of John. 26 So he began to speak boldly in the synagogue. When Aquila and Priscilla heard him, they took him aside and explained to him the way of God more accurately. 27 And when he desired to cross to Achaia, the brethren wrote, exhorting the disciples to receive him; and when he arrived, he greatly helped those who had believed through grace; 28 for he vigorously refuted the Jews publicly, showing from the Scriptures that Jesus is the Christ. 19 And it happened, while Apollos was at Corinth, that Paul, having passed through the upper regions, came to Ephesus. And finding some disciples 2 he said to them, "Did you receive the Holy Spirit when you believed?" So they said to him, "We have not so much as heard whether there is a Holy Spirit." 3 And he said to them, "Into what then were you baptized?" So they said, "Into John's baptism." 4 Then Paul said, "John indeed baptized with a baptism of repentance, saying to the people that they should believe on Him who would come after him, that is, on Christ Jesus." 5 When they heard this, they were baptized in the name of the Lord Jesus. 6 And when Paul had laid hands on them, the Holy Spirit came upon them, and they spoke with tongues and prophesied. 7 Now the men were about twelve in all. 8 And he went into the synagogue and spoke boldly for three months, reasoning and persuading concerning the things of the kingdom of God. 9 But when some were hardened and did not believe, but spoke evil of the Way before the multitude, he departed from them and withdrew the disciples, reasoning daily in the school of Tyrannus. 10 And this continued for two years, so that all who dwelt in Asia heard the word of the Lord Jesus, both Jews and Greeks. 11 Now God worked unusual miracles by the hands of Paul, 12 so that even handkerchiefs or aprons were brought from his body to the sick, and the diseases left them and the evil spirits went out of them. 13 Then some of the itinerant Jewish exorcists took it upon themselves to call the name of the Lord Jesus over those who had evil spirits, saying, "We exorcise you by the Jesus whom Paul preaches." 14 Also there were seven sons of Sceva, a Jewish chief priest, who did so. 15 And the evil spirit answered and said, "Jesus I know, and Paul I know; but who are you?" 16 Then the man in whom the evil spirit was leaped on them, overpowered them, and prevailed against them, so that they fled out of that house naked and wounded. 17 This became known both to all Jews and Greeks dwelling in Ephesus; and fear fell on them all, and the name of the Lord Jesus was magnified. 18 And many who had believed came confessing and telling their deeds. 19 Also, many of those who had practiced magic brought their books together and burned them in the sight of all. And they counted up the value of them, and it totaled fifty thousand pieces of silver. 20 So the word of the Lord grew mightily and prevailed. 21 When these things were accomplished, Paul purposed in the Spirit, when he had passed through Macedonia and Achaia, to go to Jerusalem, saying, "After I have been there, I must also see Rome." 22 So he sent into Macedonia two of those who ministered to him, Timothy and Erastus, but he himself stayed in Asia for a time. 23 And about that time there arose a great commotion about the Way. 24 For a certain man named Demetrius, a silversmith, who made silver shrines of Diana, brought no small profit to the craftsmen. 25 He called them together with the workers of similar occupation, and said: "Men, you know that we have our prosperity by this trade. 26 Moreover you see and hear that not only at Ephesus, but throughout almost all Asia, this Paul has persuaded and turned away many people, saying that they are not gods which are made with hands. 27 So not only is this trade of ours in danger of falling into disrepute, but also the temple of the great goddess Diana may be despised and her magnificence destroyed, whom all Asia and the world worship." 28 Now when they heard this, they were full of wrath and cried out, saying, "Great is Diana of the Ephesians!" 29 So the whole city was filled with confusion, and rushed into the theater with one accord, having seized Gaius and Aristarchus, Macedonians, Paul's travel companions. 30 And when Paul wanted to go in to the people, the disciples would not allow him. 31 Then some of the officials of Asia, who were his friends, sent to him pleading that he would not venture into the theater. 32 Some therefore cried one thing and some another, for the assembly was confused, and most of them did not know why they had come together. 33 And they drew Alexander out of the multitude, the Jews putting him forward. And Alexander motioned with his hand, and wanted to make his defense to the people. 34 But when they found out that he was a Jew, all with one voice cried out for about two hours, "Great is Diana of the Ephesians!" 35 And when the city clerk had quieted the crowd, he said: "Men of Ephesus, what man is there who does not know that the city of the Ephesians is temple guardian of the great goddess Diana, and of the image which fell down from Zeus? 36 Therefore, since these things cannot be denied, you ought to be quiet and do nothing rashly. 37 For you have brought these men here who are neither robbers of temples nor blasphemers of your goddess. 38 Therefore, if Demetrius and his fellow craftsmen have a case against anyone, the courts are open and there are proconsuls. Let them bring charges against one another.*

INTRODUCTION:

A. Paul's third missionary journey began with a tour of Galatia and Phrygia. Acts 16:6 says that Paul, Silas and Timothy were forbidden by the Holy Spirit to preach the word in Asia.

B. The ministry of Apollos the Jew from Alexandria.

   1. He was an educated man - Alexandria was one of the learning centers of the world.

   2. He was eloquent in speech - in language expression

   3. He was mighty in the scriptures - he knew the word of God

   4. He was instructed in the way of the Lord - the way-Acts 9:27; 19:9,23; 22:4; 24:22

   5. He was fervent in the Spirit - on fire

   6. He taught diligently the things of God - knowing only the Baptism of John

   7. He was bold - to proclaim truth

   8. He was teachable - a sign of maturity. He swayed the crowd, but he was willing to listen to two testimonies.

   9. He preached Christ - these are the kinds of people God uses to take a city....We need to be like Apollos, Aquila and Priscilla.

C. The enemy uses weapons of accusation and deceit! II Corinthians 10:3,4

D. Let's see how a city was taken.

I. Taking A City With God's Power

A. The need of God's power

   1. Paul came to Ephesus. It was the market of Asia Minor called the "Treasure House of Asia". It had the temple of the goddess Diana. Ephesus was the center of pagan superstition. Diana was famous for her charms and spells called "Ephesian Letters". They were supposedly guaranteed to bring safety on a journey, to bring children to the childless, etc. Ephesus was a gathering place for merchants, magic workers, astrologers as well as criminals.

   2. Paul found some disciples and asked them, "Did you receive the Holy Spirit when you believed?" They told him they had not heard there was a Holy Spirit. Paul asked them what they were baptized into and they said John's baptism. The people were baptized in the name of the Lord Jesus. Paul then laid hands on them and they received the Holy Spirit, began to speak in tongues and prophesied.

   3. There were twelve men in all. Paul preached and taught for three months, reasoning and persuading them concerning the things of the Kingdom of God.

   4. Paul then withdrew himself and the disciples when some were hardened. Paul reasoned daily in the School of Tyrannus for two years to all who dwelt in Asia. They heard the word of the Lord Jesus.

B. The display of God's power

   1. God wrought special miracles by the hands of Paul.

      a. Hands = blessing

     b. Mark 16:18, *...they will lay hands on the sick, and they will recover.*
2. The itinerant Jewish exorcists and the seven sons of Sceva tried to adjure the evil spirits out in the name of the Lord Jesus.
     a. The evil spirit answered, "Jesus I know, and Paul I know, but who are you?" Then the evil spirit overcame them.
     b. When it became known to the Jews and Greeks in Ephesus fear fell on them all and the name of the Lord Jesus was magnified!
     c. Then the people confessed and told their deeds. They got rid of their occultic books.

APPLICATION:
  A. Are you saved? Are you baptized in the Holy Spirit?
  B. There is power in the Name of Jesus! God works with us. The word grew mightily and prevailed.

II. Taking A City With A Disturbance
  A. The need for a disturbance
    1. A stir was caused about the way.
    2. Demetrius, a silversmith, made money from making statues of the goddess Diana. He told the people of the city that the temple of the great goddess Diana was in trouble.
    3. They were bound to materialism and idols. Don't let money dominate you!
    4. The people cried out, "Great is Diana of the Ephesians." The whole city was in confusion. "God is not the author of confusion."
    5. They rushed the theater after seizing Gaius and Aristarchus, Paul's companions. The disciples would not let Paul go into the theater.
  B. The results of the disturbance
    1. The city clerk of Ephesus cut through the problem and told them to open the legal process if there was any inquiry or changes.
    2. We disturb practices that contradict the Kingdom of God.

APPLICATION: Are you stirring things up?

THE HEART OF PAUL

Acts 20 - *1 After the uproar had ceased, Paul called the disciples to himself, embraced them, and departed to go to Macedonia. 2 Now when he had gone over that region and encouraged them with many words, he came to Greece 3 and stayed three months. And when the Jews plotted against him as he was about to sail to Syria, he decided to return through Macedonia. 4 And Sopater of Berea accompanied him to Asia—also Aristarchus and Secundus of the Thessalonians, and Gaius of Derbe, and Timothy, and Tychicus and Trophimus of Asia. 5 These men, going ahead, waited for us at Troas. 6 But we sailed away from Philippi after the Days of Unleavened Bread, and in five days joined them at Troas, where we stayed seven days. 7 Now on the first day of the week, when the disciples came together to break bread, Paul, ready to depart the next day, spoke to them and continued his message until midnight. 8 There were many lamps in the upper room where they were gathered together. 9 And in a window sat a certain young man named Eutychus, who was sinking into a deep sleep. He was overcome by sleep; and as Paul continued speaking, he fell down from the third story and was taken up dead. 10 But Paul went down, fell on him, and embracing him said, "Do not trouble yourselves, for his life is in him." 11 Now when he had come up, had broken bread and eaten, and talked a long while, even till daybreak, he departed. 12 And they brought the young man in alive, and they were not a little comforted. 13 Then we went ahead to the ship and sailed to Assos, there intending to take Paul on board; for so he had given orders, intending himself to go on foot. 14 And when he met us at Assos, we took him on board and came to Mitylene. 15 We sailed from there, and the next day came opposite Chios. The following day we arrived at Samos and stayed at Trogyllium. The next day we came to Miletus. 16 For Paul had decided to sail past Ephesus, so that he would not have to spend time in Asia; for he was hurrying to be at Jerusalem, if possible, on the Day of Pentecost. 17 From Miletus he sent to Ephesus and called for the elders of the church. 18 And when they had come to him, he said to them: "You know, from the first day that I came to Asia, in what manner I always lived among you, 19 serving the Lord with all humility, with many tears and trials which happened to me by the plotting of the Jews; 20 how I kept back nothing that was helpful, but proclaimed it to you, and taught you publicly and from house to house, 21 testifying to Jews, and also to Greeks, repentance toward God and faith toward our Lord Jesus Christ. 22 And see, now I go bound in the spirit to Jerusalem, not knowing the things that will happen to me there, 23 except that the Holy Spirit testifies in every city, saying that chains and tribulations await me. 24 But none of these things move me; nor do I count my life dear to myself, so that I may finish my race with joy, and the ministry which I received from the Lord Jesus, to testify to the gospel of the grace of God. 25 "And indeed, now I know that you all, among whom I have gone preaching the kingdom of God, will see my face no more. 26 Therefore I testify to you this day that I am innocent of the blood of all men. 27 For I have not shunned to declare to you the whole counsel of God. 28 Therefore take heed to yourselves and to all the flock, among which the Holy Spirit has made you overseers, to shepherd the church of God which He purchased with His own blood. 29 For I know this, that after my departure savage wolves will come in among you, not sparing the flock. 30 Also from among yourselves men will rise up, speaking perverse things, to draw away the disciples after themselves. 31 Therefore watch, and remember that for three years I did not cease to warn everyone night and day with tears. 32 "So now, brethren, I commend you to God and to the word of His grace, which is able to build you up and give you an inheritance among all those who are sanctified. 33 I have coveted no one's silver or gold or apparel. 34 Yes, you yourselves know that these hands have provided for my necessities, and for those who were with me. 35 I have shown you in every way, by laboring like this, that you must support the weak. And remember the words of the Lord Jesus, that He said, 'It is more blessed to give than to receive.' " 36 And when he had said these things, he knelt down and prayed with them all. 37 Then they all wept freely, and fell on Paul's neck and kissed him, 38 sorrowing most of all for the words which he spoke, that they would see his face no more. And they accompanied him to the ship.*

INTRODUCTION:
- A. Look at what or who is at the heart of your life.
- B. "For me to live is Christ," Paul said.
- C. The heart of the matter is the heart.
- D. From this chapter on, Paul spent much time defending himself but he kept sight of his vision. "As a direct result of one of his final missionary tasks, the city of Ephesusbecame the center of world Christianity for the next 200 years."[4] - C. Peter Wagner
- E. Let's look at Paul's heart to see how God can change our hearts. Paul was a pioneer. "[Paul] looked around for fresh worlds to conquer." - F.F. Bruce

I. Paul's Heart To Help Others
- A. Paul departed after the uproar to go to Macedonia.
  1. He went to Troas first. (II Corinthians 2:12,13)
  2. He exhorted and encouraged them in Macedonia (Philippi). He was their apostolic spiritual father.
- B. Paul spent three months in Greece. He found out there was a Jewish plot to kill him so he traveled by land rather than ship.
- C. Paul had many men with him. It appeared they had the duty of taking their contributions to Jerusalem.
- D. In verse 6, the Day of Passover began and lasted a week. The Passover was a reminder to the Jews of their deliverance from Egypt. The breaking of bread was the love feast. These Christians ate in loving fellowship with one another. It marked the family–type spirit of the church.
- E. Eutychus
  1. Possibly Eutychus had a hard day's work or some how was extremely tired. He was a young man who sat by the window. He fell to the courtyard below. The picture here was a family meeting place rather than a service.
  2. Paul fell on him and embraced him. "Do not trouble yourselves, for his life is in him." They were not a little comforted.

APPLICATION:
- A. Paul took up an offering to help. He loved the family of God and desired to reach out to them.
- B. Have a love feast. We can help others. Sometimes we are more concerned about people falling out of fellowship rather than a window.

II. Paul's Heart For The Lord
- A. V13-16 - Tells more of Paul's journey. He desired to be at Jerusalem for Pentecost.
- B. Paul called the elders of the church together.
  1. He told them he was with them during all the seasons. We go through seasons in our lives.
  2. Ecclesiates 3:1 - *To everything there is a season, a time for every purpose under heaven.*
  3. Philippians 4:11-13 - *Not that I speak in regard to need, for I have learned in whatever state I am, to be content: I know how to be abased, and I know how to abound. Everywhere and in all things I have learned both to be full and to be hungry, both to abound and to suffer need. I can do all things through Christ who strengthens me.*
  4. Paul loved the Lord.
  5. He served the Lord with humility of mind.
  6. He served the Lord with many tears.
  7. He served the Lord in temptations.
  8. He kept nothing back from the elders.
  9. He taught publicly and from house to house.
  10. He testified to the Jews and Greeks about repentance toward God and faith toward the Lord Jesus Christ.
- C. Paul was a love slave.

1. He was bound in the Spirit, not knowing what would happen to him.
2. The Holy Spirit testifies in every city what bonds and afflictions awaited him.

APPLICATION: Like Paul we need and should want to love Jesus!

III. Paul's Heart For The Church

A. But none of these things moved Paul. He did not count his own life dear to himself. He wanted to finish his course with joy, and use the ministry he received from the Lord Jesus to testify of the gospel and grace of God.

B. Paul knew he would not see their faces any more.
   1. He preached the gospel of the kingdom.
   2. He was innocent of the blood of all men. Paul declared the whole counsel of God.
   3. He reminded them of their duty.
   4. Jesus shed His blood to purchase the church of God - the blood of God.
   5. Overseers - the men who watch or oversee. Paul saw from a distance. He saw the whole picture rather than a part. He was to watch and feed.

C. Paul warned of dangers from without and from within.
   1. Without - wolves entering in among you.
   2. Within - men speaking perverse things to draw away the disciples after themselves.
   3. He warned them night and day with tears.

D. Then Paul did the following three things:
   1. "So now, brethren, I commend you to God and to the word of His grace, which is able to build you up and give you an inheritance among all those who are sanctified."
      a. "I'm not what I used to be; I'm not what I ought to be; but praise the Lord, I'm on my way to becoming all that I was intended to be."[5] - Dr. Ogilvie
      b. The Word of His grace is the key to sanctification. God's grace enables us to admit our failures, have them forgiven and move toward growth in the full statue of Christ.
   2. He worked and told them Jesus said, "It is more blessed to give than to receive." When Christ lives in us growth takes place as we give ourselves away.
   3. He prayed and wept.

APPLICATION:
A. Paul loved the church.
B. He prayed and wept.
C. He cared for them.
D. He fed them.
E. He watched out for them.
F. Do you love His church?
G. Do you love His people?

LET'S GO FOR IT - WITH COURAGE

Acts 21 - *Now it came to pass, that when we had departed from them and set sail, running a straight course we came to Cos, the following day to Rhodes, and from there to Patara. 2 And finding a ship sailing over to Phoenicia, we went aboard and set sail. 3 When we had sighted Cyprus, we passed it on the left, sailed to Syria, and landed at Tyre; for there the ship was to unload her cargo. 4 And finding disciples, we stayed there seven days. They told Paul through the Spirit not to go up to Jerusalem. 5 When we had come to the end of those days, we departed and went on our way; and they all accompanied us, with wives and children, till we were out of the city. And we knelt down on the shore and prayed. 6 When we had taken our leave of one another, we boarded the ship, and they returned home. 7 And when we had finished our voyage from Tyre, we came to Ptolemais, greeted the brethren, and stayed with them one day. 8 On the next day we who were Paul's companions departed and came to Caesarea, and entered the house of Philip the evangelist, who was one of the seven, and stayed with him. 9 Now this man had four virgin daughters who prophesied. 10 And as we stayed many days, a certain prophet named Agabus came down from Judea. 11 When he had come to us, he took Paul's belt, bound his own hands and feet, and said, "Thus says the Holy Spirit, 'So shall the Jews at Jerusalem bind the man who owns this belt, and deliver him into the hands of the Gentiles.' " 12 Now when we heard these things, both we and those from that place pleaded with him not to go up to Jerusalem. 13 Then Paul answered, "What do you mean by weeping and breaking my heart? For I am ready not only to be bound, but also to die at Jerusalem for the name of the Lord Jesus." 14 So when he would not be persuaded, we ceased, saying, "The will of the Lord be done." 15 And after those days we packed and went up to Jerusalem. 16 Also some of the disciples from Caesarea went with us and brought with them a certain Mnason of Cyprus, an early disciple, with whom we were to lodge. 17 And when we had come to Jerusalem, the brethren received us gladly. 18 On the following day Paul went in with us to James, and all the elders were present. 19 When he had greeted them, he told in detail those things which God had done among the Gentiles through his ministry. 20 And when they heard it, they glorified the Lord. And they said to him, "You see, brother, how many myriads of Jews there are who have believed, and they are all zealous for the law; 21 but they have been informed about you that you teach all the Jews who are among the Gentiles to forsake Moses, saying that they ought not to circumcise their children nor to walk according to the customs. 22 What then? The assembly must certainly meet, for they will hear that you have come. 23 Therefore do what we tell you: We have four men who have taken a vow. 24 Take them and be purified with them, and pay their expenses so that they may shave their heads, and that all may know that those things of which they were informed concerning you are nothing, but that you yourself also walk orderly and keep the law. 25 But concerning the Gentiles who believe, we have written and decided that they should observe no such thing, except that they should keep themselves from things offered to idols, from blood, from things strangled, and from sexual immorality." 26 Then Paul took the men, and the next day, having been purified with them, entered the temple to announce the expiration of the days of purification, at which time an offering should be made for each one of them. 27 Now when the seven days were almost ended, the Jews from Asia, seeing him in the temple, stirred up the whole crowd and laid hands on him, 28 crying out, "Men of Israel, help! This is the man who teaches all men everywhere against the people, the law, and this place; and furthermore he also brought Greeks into the temple and has defiled this holy place." 29 (For they had previously seen Trophimus the Ephesian with him in the city, whom they supposed that Paul had brought into the temple.) 30 And all the city was disturbed; and the people ran together, seized Paul, and dragged him out of the temple; and immediately the doors were shut. 31 Now as they were seeking to kill him, news came to the commander of the garrison that all Jerusalem was in an uproar. 32 He immediately took soldiers and centurions, and ran down to them. And when they saw the commander and the soldiers, they stopped beating Paul. 33 Then the commander came near and took him, and commanded him to be bound with two chains; and he asked who he was and what he had done. 34 And some among the multitude cried one thing and some another. So when he could not ascertain the truth because of the tumult, he commanded him to be taken into the barracks. 35 When he reached the stairs, he had to be carried by the soldiers because of the violence of the mob. 36 For the multitude of the people followed after, crying out, "Away with him!" 37 Then as Paul was about to be led into the barracks, he said to the commander, "May I speak to you?" He replied, "Can you speak Greek? 38 Are you not the Egyptian who some time ago stirred up a rebellion and led the four thousand assassins out into the wilderness?" 39 But Paul said, "I am a Jew from Tarsus, in Cilicia, a citizen of no mean city; and I implore you, permit me to speak to the people." 40 So when he had given him permission, Paul stood on the stairs and motioned with his hand to the people. And when there was a great silence, he spoke to them in the Hebrew language, saying,*

INTRODUCTION
Go for it illustration.

A. Acts 20:22-23 - *And see, now I go bound in the spirit to Jerusalem, not knowing the things that will happen to me there, except that the Holy Spirit testifies in every city, saying that chains and tribulations await me.*

B. One of America's leading market researchers said, "Don't forget the needs of people. They are living with tremendous stress and they need courage. Just know this: when you help them to live courageously, you will always be on target."

C. Let's look at the courage Paul needed to face hardships and criticism in his life and how it can be applied to ours.

I. **The Courage To Face Hardships In Going For It**

A. Paul presses on
   1. Through his travels, Paul landed at Tyre. There he found disciples and stayed there seven days.
   2. The words "and finding disciples" means a searching out. Paul had to look diligently. He found courage throughout his life, through relationship with the family of God.

B. Paul faces discouragement
   1. They told him not to go up to Jerusalem.
   2. Along our walk with the Lord people will seek to tell us different things. Keep going for it! The Greek word dia = "as a consequence" of what the Spirit had told them.
   3. They knelt down and prayed.

C. Paul gets encouraged
   1. He came to Caesarea to the house of Philip the evangelist, or the deacon. Philip had four virgin daughters that prophesied.
   2. What is truly amazing is that about 20 years later Philip and Paul, who had been Saul, were transformed from enemies to brothers in Christ.

D. The prophecy spoken over Paul challenged him about his need for courage.
   1. A prophet from Judea named Agabus came and bound his own hands and feet with Paul's belt. He told Paul that the person who owns this belt would be delivered to the gentiles.
   2. When people heard of these things they pleaded for Paul not to go up to Jerusalem.
   3. Paul said, "What do you mean by weeping and breaking My heart? For I am ready not only to be bound, but also to die at Jerusalem for the name of the Lord Jesus." And when Paul would not be persuaded, his travel companions said, "the will of the Lord be done."
      a. Breaking here does not mean suffering, weakening or bending, but attempting to weaken Paul's purpose.
      b. Paul is right. The test of motive; the motive of the church was love for the Lord.

       c. The Spirit of the Lord gave the prophecy that hardships and imprisonment were ahead. Their prophesy was colored by their own personality and desire.

       d. Go for God's best. Even if you have failed.

APPLICATION:

1. Is anything discouraging going on?
2. Is any discouraging being done?
3. Let the will of God be done, not your own desire. Go for it!
4. Judge prophecy
    a. Be open-you must obey God!
    b. We know in part and prophecy in part.
    c. Prophecy involves revelation, interpretation and application.

II. Courage To Face Criticism In Going For It

A. They went to Jerusalem to report
   1. The brethren gladly received them.
   2. Paul brought an offering and gave testimony to what God had done.
B. They came to Jerusalem and were confronted with criticism.
   1. The Jews heard that they were gold to forsake Moses' law and not circumcise their children.
   2. Paul sponsored four men which took a special kind of greatness and courage. Paul was able to compromise for unity without sacrificing his union with Christ. Secondary things did not matter because ultimately his commitment was to Christ.
   3. Most of us are able to withstand criticism from our protagonists or enemies. It is when fellow Christians criticize us that we are deeply hurt. We need a special quality of courage from the Lord.
   4. The Asian Jews stirred up the people and laid hands on Paul. They falsely accused him. They drew Paul out of the temple and were going to kill him, but a soldier saved him when he heard him speak Greek.

APPLICATION:

A. Trace criticism to it's real source. Proverbs 14:15 - *The simple believes every word, but the prudent considers well his steps.*
B. Respond quickly and wisely to your critics. James 3:5 - *Even so the tongue is a little member and boasts great things. See how great a forest a little fire kindles!* Stop the forest fires!
C. Know that your message and calling are from God. Galatians 6:4 - *But let each one examine his own work, and then he will have rejoicing in himself alone, and not in another.*
D. Encourage your heart in the Lord. I Samuel 30:6 - *Now David was greatly distressed, for the people spoke of stoning him, because the soul of all the people was grieved, every man for his sons and his daughters. But David strengthened himself in the LORD his God.*
E. Look at fear as an invitation to defeat. II Timothy 1:7 - *For God has not given us a spirit of fear, but of power and of love and of a sound mind."*
F. Let God confirm your ministry. I Peter 5:10-11 - *But may the God of all grace, who called us to His eternal glory by Christ Jesus, after you have suffered a while, perfect, establish, strengthen, and settle you. To Him be the glory and the dominion forever and ever. Amen.*
G. Matthew 5:12 - *Rejoice and be exceedingly glad, for great is your reward in heaven, for so they persecuted the prophets who were before you.* Thank God - as Paul was courageous, we can be courageous. Go for it!

BORN FREE & BREAK FREE

Acts 22 - *"Brethren and fathers, hear my defense before you now." 2 And when they heard that he spoke to them in the Hebrew language, they kept all the more silent. Then he said: 3 "I am indeed a Jew, born in Tarsus of Cilicia, but brought up in this city at the feet of Gamaliel, taught according to the strictness of our fathers' law, and was zealous toward God as you all are today. 4 I persecuted this Way to the death, binding and delivering into prisons both men and women, 5 as also the high priest bears me witness, and all the council of the elders, from whom I also received letters to the brethren, and went to Damascus to bring in chains even those who were there to Jerusalem to be punished. 6 "Now it happened, as I journeyed and came near Damascus at about noon, suddenly a great light from heaven shone around me. 7 And I fell to the ground and heard a voice saying to me, 'Saul, Saul, why are you persecuting Me?' 8 So I answered, 'Who are You, Lord?' And He said to me, 'I am Jesus of Nazareth, whom you are persecuting.' 9 "And those who were with me indeed saw the light and were afraid, but they did not hear the voice of Him who spoke to me. 10 So I said, 'What shall I do, Lord?' And the Lord said to me, 'Arise and go into Damascus, and there you will be told all things which are appointed for you to do.' 11 And since I could not see for the glory of that light, being led by the hand of those who were with me, I came into Damascus. 12 "Then a certain Ananias, a devout man according to the law, having a good testimony with all the Jews who dwelt there, 13 came to me; and he stood and said to me, 'Brother Saul, receive your sight.' And at that same hour I looked up at him. 14 Then he said, 'The God of our fathers has chosen you that you should know His will, and see the Just One, and hear the voice of His mouth. 15 For you will be His witness to all men of what you have seen and heard. 16 And now why are you waiting? Arise and be baptized, and wash away your sins, calling on the name of the Lord.' 17 "Now it happened, when I returned to Jerusalem and was praying in the temple, that I was in a trance 18 and saw Him saying to me, 'Make haste and get out of Jerusalem quickly, for they will not receive your testimony concerning Me.' 19 So I said, 'Lord, they know that in every synagogue I imprisoned and beat those who believe on You. 20 And when the blood of Your martyr Stephen was shed, I also was standing by consenting [b]to his death, and guarding the clothes of those who were killing him.' 21 Then He said to me, 'Depart, for I will send you far from here to the Gentiles.' " 22 And they listened to him until this word, and then they raised their voices and said, 'Away with such a fellow from the earth, for he is not fit to live!" 23 Then, as they cried out and tore off their clothes and threw dust into the air, 24 the commander ordered him to be brought into the barracks, and said that he should be examined under scourging, so that he might know why they shouted so against him. 25 And as they bound him with thongs, Paul said to the centurion who stood by, "Is it lawful for you to scourge a man who is a Roman, and uncondemned?" 26 When the centurion heard that, he went and told the commander, saying, "Take care what you do, for this man is a Roman." 27 Then the commander came and said to him, "Tell me, are you a Roman?" He said, "Yes." 28 The commander answered, "With a large sum I obtained this citizenship." And Paul said, "But I was born a citizen." 29 Then immediately those who were about to examine him withdrew from him; and the commander was also afraid after he found out that he was a Roman, and because he had bound him. 30 The next day, because he wanted to know for certain why he was accused by the Jews, he released him from his bonds, and commanded the chief priests and all their council to appear, and brought Paul down and set him before them.*

INTRODUCTION
A. Are you born free? Paul spoke of his two births.
B. "If you are born once you will die twice, if you are born twice you will die once."
C. Do you need to break free or do you need to be born free?
D. Let's look at breaking free from the past and breaking free in the present.

I. Breaking Free From The Past
A. Paul shared his past.
   1. He spoke to them in the Hebrew tongue which attracted attention. He shared his personal experiences. His audience probably contained Messianic Jews and unbelieving Jews.
   2. Paul told how he was a Jew born in Tarsus, a student trained at Gamaliel's feet. He persecuted this way unto death and put people in prison.
      a. He did all these things because he thought he was doing right.
      b. Philippians 3:3-11 - *For we are the circumcision, who worship God in the Spirit, rejoice in Christ Jesus, and have no confidence in the flesh, though I also might have confidence in the flesh. If anyone else thinks he may have confidence in the flesh, I more so: circumcised the eighth day, of the stock of Israel, of the tribe of Benjamin, a Hebrew of the Hebrews; concerning the law, a Pharisee; concerning zeal, persecuting the church; concerning the righteousness which is in the law, blameless. But what things were gain to me, these I have counted loss for Christ. Yet indeed I also count all things loss for the excellence of the knowledge of Christ Jesus my Lord, for whom I have suffered the loss of all things, and count them as rubbish, that I may gain Christ and be found in Him, not having my own righteousness, which is from the law, but that which is through faith in Christ, the righteousness which is from God by faith; that I may know Him and the power of His resurrection, and the fellowship of His sufferings, being conformed to His death, if, by any means, I may attain to the resurrection from the dead.*
B. Jesus broke into his past.
   1. Christ confronted Saul on the road to Damascus. Saul fell to the ground when a great light shown all around him.
   2. Christ said, "Saul! Saul, why are you persecuting me? I am Jesus of Nazareth whom you are persecuting."
   3. He told Saul to arise and go into Damascus. The glory of the light blinded him. Those that were with Saul lead him by the hand. Ananias prayed for Saul and he received his sight.
   4. Saul was born again! (John 3) Christ told him to be baptized and to go on. He was there at Stephen's death. God drew him and forgave him.
   5. Saul was chosen: first to know His will, second to see the Just One and third to hear His voice.

APPLICATION
A. Has Jesus broken into your past?
B. Have you begun a new life?
C. He wants to break us free!
D. You have a personal testimony!

II. BREAKING FREE IN THE PRESENT
A. Problems in Paul's present
   1. "Depart for I will send you to the 'Gentiles'." What word would it have been for you or me? The Jews got angry when Paul said the word "Gentiles."
   2. The Jews cast off their garments and threw dust in the air.
   3. The chief captain commanded Paul to be brought into the castle and examined him by scourging.
      a. They bound Paul with thongs, meaning they stretched him forward, beat him and tied him to a post. Paul said, "Is it lawful for you to scourge a man who is a Roman, and uncondemned?" No wonder the penalty for scourging a Roman citizen was death.
      b. The commander (Claudius Lysias - Acts 23:26) most likely had to pay a great sum to buy Paul's citizenship. Paul said, "But I was born a citizen."
      c. Christ controls the circumstances in our lives, just as He had this commander at the right place. Christ brought him to the council.

B. Problems in your Present.
1. Are you trapped?
2. He loves you!
3. Let Him break you out of the old. New wine goes into new wineskins.

APPLICATION
A. Let Him break you free!
B. Galatians 5:1 - *Stand fast therefore in the liberty by which Christ has made us free, and do not be entangled again with a yoke of bondage.*
C. II Corinthians 3:16-18 - *Nevertheless when one turns to the Lord, the veil is taken away. Now the Lord is the Spirit; and where the Spirit of the Lord is, there is liberty. But we all, with unveiled face, beholding as in a mirror the glory of the Lord, are being transformed into the same image from glory to glory, just as by the Spirit of the Lord.*

THE LORD STANDS WITH YOU

Acts 23 - Then Paul, looking earnestly at the council, said, "Men and brethren, I have lived in all good conscience before God until this day." 2 And the high priest Ananias commanded those who stood by him to strike him on the mouth. 3 Then Paul said to him, "God will strike you, you whitewashed wall! For you sit to judge me according to the law, and do you command me to be struck contrary to the law?" 4 And those who stood by said, "Do you revile God's high priest?" 5 Then Paul said, "I did not know, brethren, that he was the high priest; for it is written, 'You shall not speak evil of a ruler of your people.' " 6 But when Paul perceived that one part were Sadducees and the other Pharisees, he cried out in the council, "Men and brethren, I am a Pharisee, the son of a Pharisee; concerning the hope and resurrection of the dead I am being judged!" 7 And when he had said this, a dissension arose between the Pharisees and the Sadducees; and the assembly was divided. 8 For Sadducees say that there is no resurrection—and no angel or spirit; but the Pharisees confess both. 9 Then there arose a loud outcry. And the scribes of the Pharisees' party arose and protested, saying, "We find no evil in this man; but if a spirit or an angel has spoken to him, let us not fight against God." 10 Now when there arose a great dissension, the commander, fearing lest Paul might be pulled to pieces by them, commanded the soldiers to go down and take him by force from among them, and bring him into the barracks. 11 But the following night the Lord stood by him and said, "Be of good cheer, Paul; for as you have testified for Me in Jerusalem, so you must also bear witness at Rome." 12 And when it was day, some of the Jews banded together and bound themselves under an oath, saying that they would neither eat nor drink till they had killed Paul. 13 Now there were more than forty who had formed this conspiracy. 14 They came to the chief priests and elders, and said, "We have bound ourselves under a great oath that we will eat nothing until we have killed Paul. 15 Now you, therefore, together with the council, suggest to the commander that he be brought down to you tomorrow, as though you were going to make further inquiries concerning him; but we are ready to kill him before he comes near." 16 So when Paul's sister's son heard of their ambush, he went and entered the barracks and told Paul. 17 Then Paul called one of the centurions to him and said, "Take this young man to the commander, for he has something to tell him." 18 So he took him and brought him to the commander and said, "Paul the prisoner called me to him and asked me to bring this young man to you. He has something to say to you." 19 Then the commander took him by the hand, went aside, and asked privately, "What is it that you have to tell me?" 20 And he said, "The Jews have agreed to ask that you bring Paul down to the council tomorrow, as though they were going to inquire more fully about him. 21 But do not yield to them, for more than forty of them lie in wait for him, men who have bound themselves by an oath that they will neither eat nor drink till they have killed him; and now they are ready, waiting for the promise from you." 22 So the commander let the young man depart, and commanded him, "Tell no one that you have revealed these things to me." 23 And he called for two centurions, saying, "Prepare two hundred soldiers, seventy horsemen, and two hundred spearmen to go to Caesarea at the third hour of the night; 24 and provide mounts to set Paul on, and bring him safely to Felix the governor." 25 He wrote a letter in the following manner: 26 Claudius Lysias, To the most excellent governor Felix: Greetings. 27 This man was seized by the Jews and was about to be killed by them. Coming with the troops I rescued him, having learned that he was a Roman. 28 And when I wanted to know the reason they accused him, I brought him before their council. 29 I found out that he was accused concerning questions of their law, but had nothing charged against him deserving of death or chains. 30 And when it was told me that the Jews lay in wait for the man, I sent him immediately to you, and also commanded his accusers to state before you the charges against him. Farewell. 31 Then the soldiers, as they were commanded, took Paul and brought him by night to Antipatris. 32 The next day they left the horsemen to go on with him, and returned to the barracks. 33 When they came to Caesarea and had delivered the letter to the governor, *they also presented Paul to him. 34 And when the governor had read it, he asked what province he was from. And when he understood that he was from Cilicia, 35 he said, "I will hear you when your accusers also have come." And he commanded him to be kept in Herod's Praetorium.*

INTRODUCTION

A. The Bible talks much about standing.

B. Exodus 14:13-14 - *And Moses said to the people, 'Do not be afraid. Stand still, and see the salvation of the Lord, which He will accomplish for you today. For the Egyptians whom you see today, you shall see again no more forever. The Lord will fight for you, and you shall hold your peace.'*

C. Ephesians 6:12 - *Having done all to stand, stand in the evil day.*

D. I Peter 6:12 - *By Silas, a faithful brother unto you, as I suppose, I have written briefly exhorting and testifying that this is the true grace of God wherein ye stand.*

E. Let's look at how the Lord wants to stand with you in your humanity, in your trials, and until the end - to take courage and strength.

I. He Stands With You In Your Humanity.

A. We see Paul's humanity
  1. He tells the counsel that he has lived in good conscience before God.
  2. The high priest Ananias commanded them that stood by him to smite him on the mouth. Paul retaliates by calling him a whitened wall because the law says, "He who strikes the cheek of an Israelite, strikes as it were the glory of God." Then they that stood by said, "Do you revile the high priest so and he said he did not know that he was the high priest. Exodus 22:28 - *It is a crime to speak evil of the ruler of the people.*
  3. Luke exposed the human frailties of the Apostle.
  4. We have human frailties. Jesus understands our weaknesses. Hebrews 4:14-16 - *Seeing then that we have a great High Priest who has passed through the heavens, Jesus the Son of God, let us hold fast our confession. For we do not have a High Priest who cannot sympathize with our weaknesses, but was in all points tempted as we are, yet without sin. Let us therefore come boldly to the throne of grace, that we may obtain mercy and find grace to help in time of need.*
     a. Jesus understands. He is touched.
     b. You can come boldly to the throne of grace. God's kindness.
     c. Obtain mercy and find grace to help in the time of need, when you have it all together.

B. We see Paul's humility.
  1. He perceives that he is wrong and admits it. They were both wrong, but Paul admitted his mistakes.
  2. It is important to admit our mistakes.
  3. "Humility is admitting that we are people in process. "[6] - Dr. Lloyd Ogilvie
  4. 1 Peter 5:5-7 - *Likewise you younger people, submit yourselves to your elders. Yes, all of you be submissive to one another, and be clothed with humility, for "God resists the proud, but gives grace to the humble." Therefore humble yourselves under the mighty hand of God, that He may exalt you in due time, casting all your care upon Him, for He cares for you.*

C. We see Paul's hope.
  1. He perceived part were Saducees and Pharisees He said, "I am a Pharisee, etc." and said in the hope of resurrection of the dead he was called in questions.
  2. He brought the issue out in the open. He wanted to witness of the resurrection fo Christ. God gives us hope. The Pharisees believed in the resurrection, angels, etc. The Saducees did not.
  3. Sometimes we can lose our hope. Read Romans 4:17-21. Men disappoint, but God can help.
  4. Matthew 12:20- *A bruised reed shall he not break and smoking flax shall he not quench, till he sent forth judgement unto victory.*

APPLICATION: The Lord understands our humanity. His strength is perfected in our weakness. His grace is sufficient.

II. He Stands With You In Your Trials.

    A. The Lord stands with paul.

        1. They tried to pull him in pieces.

        2. He must have been discouraged.

        3. That night the Lord stood by him. He stands by you. He said, "Be of good cheer; of good courage." He gave him hope.

    B. The Lord Protects Paul.

        1. The Jews banded together to kill Paul. They made an oath - 40 of them.

        2. Paul's sisters' son heard of their lying in wait and told Paul. He told him to go to the chief captain. He tells him. Then 470 are sent to protect him. The Lord arranged the details to take care of this.

        3. The Lord protects us. But you say this happened or that happened. yes, there is sin and evil in the world, but God can love and help us. He understands.

        4. Read 2 Timothy 4:16-18

APPLICATION: God will protect you. God will see you through the trial.

III. He Stands With You Until The End.

    A. He sees Paul through the trial.

        1. They do not get him. He had warned him or hardships.

        2. The governor to whom Paul was taken to was Felix. The seat of the Roman government was not in Jerusalem but in Caesarea. It was 60 miles from Jerusalem to Caesarea and Antipatris was 25 miles from Caesarea. He ends up in Herod's judgement hall.

        3. "Beneath the appearances of the impossibilities we face, the Lord is working to press on to do His will."

    B. He saw Paul through to the end.

        1. Paul fought the good fight of faith.

        2. Hebrews 13:5 - *He will never leave nor forsake us.*

        3. Philippians 1:6 - *Being confident of this very thing, that He who has begun a good work in you will complete it until the day of Jesus Christ.*

APPLICATION: Be patient. God isn't finished with you yet. He is working in you. He loves you. He will stand with you.

DECISIONS

Acts 24 - *Now after five days Ananias the high priest came down with the elders and a certain orator named Tertullus. These gave evidence to the governor against Paul. 2 And when he was called upon, Tertullus began his accusation, saying: "Seeing that through you we enjoy great peace, and prosperity is being brought to this nation by your foresight, 3 we accept it always and in all places, most noble Felix, with all thankfulness. 4 Nevertheless, not to be tedious to you any further, I beg you to hear, by your courtesy, a few words from us. 5 For we have found this man a plague, a creator of dissension among all the Jews throughout the world, and a ringleader of the sect of the Nazarenes. 6 He even tried to profane the temple, and we seized him, and wanted to judge him according to our law. 7 But the commander Lysias came by and with great violence took him out of our hands, 8 commanding his accusers to come to you. By examining him yourself you may ascertain all these things of which we accuse him." 9 And the Jews also assented, maintaining that these things were so. 10 Then Paul, after the governor had nodded to him to speak, answered: "Inasmuch as I know that you have been for many years a judge of this nation, I do the more cheerfully answer for myself, 11 because you may ascertain that it is no more than twelve days since I went up to Jerusalem to worship. 12 And they neither found me in the temple disputing with anyone nor inciting the crowd, either in the synagogues or in the city. 13 Nor can they prove the things of which they now accuse me. 14 But this I confess to you, that according to the Way which they call a sect, so I worship the God of my fathers, believing all things which are written in the Law and in the Prophets. 15 I have hope in God, which they themselves also accept, that there will be a resurrection of the dead, both of the just and the unjust. 16 This being so, I myself always strive to have a conscience without offense toward God and men. 17 "Now after many years I came to bring alms and offerings to my nation, 18 in the midst of which some Jews from Asia found me purified in the temple, neither with a mob nor with tumult. 19 They ought to have been here before you to object if they had anything against me. 20 Or else let those who are here themselves say [f]if they found any wrongdoing in me while I stood before the council, 21 unless it is for this one statement which I cried out, standing among them, 'Concerning the resurrection of the dead I am being judged by you this day.'" 22 But when Felix heard these things, having more accurate knowledge of the Way, he adjourned the proceedings and said, "When Lysias the commander comes down, I will make a decision on your case." 23 So he commanded the centurion to keep Paul and to let him have liberty, and told him not to forbid any of his friends to provide for or visit him. 24 And after some days, when Felix came with his wife Drusilla, who was Jewish, he sent for Paul and heard him concerning the faith in Christ. 25 Now as he reasoned about righteousness, self-control, and the judgment to come, Felix was afraid and answered, "Go away for now; when I have a convenient time I will call for you." 26 Meanwhile he also hoped that money would be given him by Paul, [g]that he might release him. Therefore he sent for him more often and conversed with him. 27 But after two years Porcius Festus succeeded Felix; and Felix, wanting to do the Jews a favor, left Paul bound.*

INTRODUCTION

A. Great men and women are not born, they are made. Decisions are important. Decisions determine destiny.

B. Not to decide is to decide!

C. Let's look at the decisions made in Acts 24 and how it can help us to follow the Lord.

I. The Decision To Persecute Paul

A. Tertullus flatters Felix.

1. Ananias, the high priest, the elders and Tertullus are the ones who informed the governor to move against Paul.

2. Tertullus uses flattery. "Seeing that through you we enjoy great peace, and prosperity is being brought to this nation by your foresight, we accept it always and in all places, most noble Felix, with all thankfulness." (v2)
   a. Proverbs 28:23 - *He who rebukes a man will find more favor afterward. Than he who flatters with the tongue.*
   b. Psalm 12:3 - *May the LORD cut off all flattering lips, and the tongue that speaks proud things...*

B. Tertullus makes charges against Paul.
   1. He asks Felix to listen to the charges even though they will be tedious.
   2. It is important to realize that Felix was a complicated mixture of Roman training and spiritual curiosity. His brother Pallas was a favorite of Nero. Through his family's influence he arose from slavery to be a Roman governor. Tacitus, the Roman historian said, "He exercised the prerogatives of a king with the spirit of a slave." He was married at this time to Drusilla, the daughter of Herod Agrippa I. Greed and lust for power kept foes out of his path. He was in danger of losing his place because of his treatment to the Jews.
   3. Tertullus, the lawyer, accuses Paul of these things:
      a. He said Paul was a pestilence or a plague. Tertullus was calling Paul a pest. It was a very demeaning statement. He said that Paul was a mover of sedition throughout the whole world among the Jews. Paul was being charged as a creator of dissension.
      b. He said Paul was a ringleader of the sect of the Nazarenes. A ringleader (protostaten) means head, leader champion or instigator of action.
      c. He said Paul was a defiler of the temple and they had taken him to judge him according to their law. But Lysias the commander took him away. All the Jews agreed with him.

APPLICATION:
A. Some people choose to see falsely only from their perception.
B. That is why we need on another. We can be falsely accused.

II. The Decision To Defend Himself
A. Paul deals with the charges.
   1. Paul told Tertullas he was glad to speak to Felix. He told him they can not prove any of these things. Paul did not defile the temple or cause the problems they accused him of doing.
   2. Paul told Felix he believed in the God of his fathers, which they called a sect, and that he believed in the Law of the Prophets.
   3. He told Felix he has hope in God that there shall be a resurrection of the dead, the just and unjust.
B. Paul's decision is declared.
   1. "This being so, I myself always strive to have a conscience without offense toward God or Men."
      a. Matthew 18:15-17 - *Moreover if your brother sins against you, go and tellhim his fault between you and him alone. If he hears you, you have gained your brother. But if he will not hear, take with you one or two more, that 'by the mouth of two or three witnesses every word may be established.' And if he refuses to hear them, tell it to the church. But if he refuses even to hear the church, let him be to you like a heathen and a tax collector.*
      b. I John 3:19-21 - *And by this we know that we are of the truth, and shall assure our hearts before Him. For if our heart condemns us, God is greater than our heart, and knows all things. Beloved, if our heart does not condemn us, we have confidence toward God.*
   2. This is a good decision to make. Integrity and honesty are important. Paul told the truth about bring alms to the temple. There were no witnesses to accuse him.
   3. Paul was standing there because of the teaching of the resurrection of the dead.
   4. Felix commanded them to wait until Lysias came before he made a decision. Felix had knowledge of The Way.
   5. Felix did let Paul's friends come visit him and minister to him.

APPLICATION

    A. Seek to have a clear conscience.

    B. God does not condemn us. He loves to free us. He is greater than our hearts.

    C. Make the right decision!

III. The Decision Of Felix And Drusilla

    A. Paul challenges them with a great decision.

        1. After certain days Felix and Drusilla, who was a Jewess, sent for Paul to hear him concerning the faith in Christ.

        2. Paul reasoned:

            a. righteousness - righteousness in Christ

            b. self-control - in those who trust Him

            c. judgment to come - He will judge

        3. They probably did not anticipate the implications and the cutting edge of judgment. They were convicted.

    B. They chose not to decide.

        1. "Go away for now; when I have a convenient time I will call for you." The "don't call me I'll call you" attitude. Go away for now. Are you putting off the Lord? "We make decisions and then our decisions turn around on us."

            a. The Lord may be pressing someone to come to Him and be forgiven.

            b. He may be pressing some to be more outgoing in sharing their faith.

            c. He may be pressing some to trust Him in the biblical admonition to tithe and give.

            d. He may be pressing other to get involved in ministry.

            e. He may be pressing others to forgive themselves and others.

            f. He may be pressing some to let Him touch their hearts and begin the process. He loves us!

        2. Felix had hoped for money. He left Paul bound to please the Jews and save himself.

APPLICATION

    A. Don't say, "Go away" to the Lord. Decide!

    B. Great men and great women make great decisions!

BOOK OF ACTS SERIES | LESSON 28
THE CALL OF GOD

Acts 25 & 26 - Now when Festus had come to the province, after three days he went up from Caesarea to Jerusalem. 2 Then the high priest and the chief men of the Jews informed him against Paul; and they petitioned him, 3 asking a favor against him, that he would summon him to Jerusalem—while they lay in ambush along the road to kill him. 4 But Festus answered that Paul should be kept at Caesarea, and that he himself was going there shortly. 5 "Therefore," he said, "let those who have authority among you go down with me and accuse this man, to see if there is any fault in him." 6 And when he had remained among them more than ten days, he went down to Caesarea. And the next day, sitting on the judgment seat, he commanded Paul to be brought. 7 When he had come, the Jews who had come down from Jerusalem stood about and laid many serious complaints against Paul, which they could not prove, 8 while he answered for himself, "Neither against the law of the Jews, nor against the temple, nor against Caesar have I offended in anything at all." 9 But Festus, wanting to do the Jews a favor, answered Paul and said, "Are you willing to go up to Jerusalem and there be judged before me concerning these things?" 10 So Paul said, "I stand at Caesar's judgment seat, where I ought to be judged. To the Jews I have done no wrong, as you very well know. 11 For if I am an offender, or have committed anything deserving of death, I do not object to dying; but if there is nothing in these things of which these men accuse me, no one can deliver me to them. I appeal to Caesar." 12 Then Festus, when he had conferred with the council, answered, "You have appealed to Caesar? To Caesar you shall go!" 13 And after some days King Agrippa and Bernice came to Caesarea to greet Festus. 14 When they had been there many days, Festus laid Paul's case before the king, saying: "There is a certain man left a prisoner by Felix, 15 about whom the chief priests and the elders of the Jews informed me, when I was in Jerusalem, asking for a judgment against him. 16 To them I answered, 'It is not the custom of the Romans to deliver any man to destruction before the accused meets the accusers face to face, and has opportunity to answer for himself concerning the charge against him.' 17 Therefore when they had come together, without any delay, the next day I sat on the judgment seat and commanded the man to be brought in. 18 When the accusers stood up, they brought no accusation against him of such things as I supposed, 19 but had some questions against him about their own religion and about a certain Jesus, who had died, whom Paul affirmed to be alive. 20 And because I was uncertain of such questions, I asked whether he was willing to go to Jerusalem and there be judged concerning these matters. 21 But when Paul appealed to be reserved for the decision of Augustus, I commanded him to be kept till I could send him to Caesar." 22 Then Agrippa said to Festus, "I also would like to hear the man myself." "Tomorrow," he said, "you shall hear him." 23 So the next day, when Agrippa and Bernice had come with great pomp, and had entered the auditorium with the commanders and the prominent men of the city, at Festus' command Paul was brought in. 24 And Festus said: "King Agrippa and all the men who are here present with us, you see this man about whom the whole assembly of the Jews petitioned me, both at Jerusalem and here, crying out that he was not fit to live any longer. 25 But when I found that he had committed nothing deserving of death, and that he himself had appealed to Augustus, I decided to send him. 26 I have nothing certain to write to my lord concerning him. Therefore I have brought him out before you, and especially before you, King Agrippa, so that after the examination has taken place I may have something to write. 27 For it seems to me unreasonable to send a prisoner and not to specify the charges against him." 26 1 Then Agrippa said to Paul, "You are permitted to speak for yourself." So Paul stretched out his hand and answered for himself: 2 "I think myself happy, King Agrippa, because today I shall answer for myself before you concerning all the things of which I am accused by the Jews, 3 especially because you are expert in all customs and questions which have to do with the Jews. Therefore I beg you to hear me patiently. 4 "My manner of life from my youth, which was spent from the beginning among my own nation at Jerusalem, all the Jews know. 5 They knew me from the first, if they were willing to testify, that according to the strictest sect of our religion I lived a Pharisee. 6 And now I stand and am judged for the hope of the promise made by God to our fathers. 7 To this promise our twelve tribes, earnestly serving God night and day, hope to attain. For this hope's sake, King Agrippa, I am accused by the Jews. 8 Why should it be thought incredible by you that God raises the dead? 9 "Indeed, I myself thought I must do many things contrary to the name of Jesus of Nazareth. 10 This I also did in Jerusalem, and many of the saints I shut up in prison, having received authority from the chief priests; and when they were put to death, I cast my vote against them. 11 And I punished them often in every synagogue and compelled them to blaspheme; and being exceedingly enraged against them, I persecuted them even to foreign cities. 12 "While thus occupied, as I journeyed to Damascus with authority and commission from the chief priests, 13 at midday, O king, along the road I saw a light from heaven, brighter than the sun, shining around me and those who journeyed with me. 14 And when we all had fallen to the ground, I heard a voice speaking to me and saying in the Hebrew language, 'Saul, Saul, why are you persecuting Me? It is hard for you to kick against the goads.' 15 So I said, 'Who are You, Lord?' And He said, 'I am Jesus, whom you are persecuting. 16 But rise and stand on your feet; for I have appeared to you for this purpose, to make you a minister and a witness both of the things which you have seen and of the things which I will yet reveal to you. 17 I will deliver you from the Jewish people, as well as from the Gentiles, to whom I now send you, 18 to open their eyes, in order to turn them from darkness to light, and from the power of Satan to God, that they may receive forgiveness of sins and an inheritance among those who are sanctified by faith in Me.' 19 "Therefore, King Agrippa, I was not disobedient to the heavenly vision, 20 but declared first to those in Damascus and in Jerusalem, and throughout all the region of Judea, and then to the Gentiles, that they should repent, turn to God, and do works befitting repentance. 21 For these reasons the Jews seized me in the temple and tried to kill me. 22 Therefore, having obtained help from God, to this day I stand, witnessing both to small and great, saying no other things than those which the prophets and Moses said would come– 23 that the Christ would suffer, that He would be the first to rise from the dead, and would proclaim light to the Jewish people and to the Gentiles." 24 Now as he thus made his defense, Festus said with a loud voice, "Paul, you are beside yourself! Much learning is driving you mad!" 25 But he said, "I am not mad, most noble Festus, but speak the words of truth and reason. 26 For the king, before whom I also speak freely, knows these things; for I am convinced that none of these things escapes his attention, since this thing was not done in a corner. 27 King Agrippa, do you believe the prophets? I know that you do believe." 28 Then Agrippa said to Paul, "You almost persuade me to become a Christian." 29 And Paul said, "I would to God that not only you, but also all who hear me today, might become both almost and altogether such as I am, except for these chains." 30 When he had said these things, the king stood up, as well as the governor and Bernice and those who sat with them; 31 and when they had gone aside, they talked among themselves, saying, "This man is doing nothing deserving of death or chains." 32 Then Agrippa said to Festus, "This man might have been set free if he had not appealed to Caesar."

INTRODUCTION:

A. Festus was a different type from Felix. We know very little about him, but what we do know proves that he was a just and upright man. He died after only two years in office with an untainted name.

B. Festus was a Roman. He had an instinct for justice. He had no desire to go up against the Jews in the first days of his governorship. He offered a compromise.

C. When Paul appealed to Caesar, Festus had no choice.

D. Matthew 10:18, "You will be brought before governors and kings for My sake, as a testimony to them and to the Gentiles."

E. Agrippa and Bernice had come with great pomp. With all the Roman ceremony, in came Paul, the tent maker with his hands in chains.

F. Read Acts 26:1-32

G. Background:

    1. Paul was given permission to speak to Agrippa. He had a courteous introduction. He made mention of Agrippa's knowledge. He asked that Agrippa would listen to him patiently. (v.1-3)

2. Paul then shared his past in the Jewish faith and the hope of the resurrection. He asked Agrippa, " Why should it be thought incredible by you that God raises the dead?" Look at the flowers! (v. 4-8)
3. Paul then told his testimony, it was in harmony with Moses and the Prophets. (v. 20-23)
4. Festus then thought Paul was mad from too much learning. Paul almost convinced them to be Christians.
5. Paul, the chained prisoner, was the dominating person in this scene. Agrippa was more on trial then Paul.

I. Paul Contrary To Christ (V9-12)
A. Contrary - en an tee'os = opposite, antagonistic or against. He had done terrible things contrary to the name of Jesus of Nazareth.
B. Paul had shut up many saints in prison under the authority of the chief priests. He testified to have people punished.
C. He punished saints in every synagogue and compelled them to blaspheme. Paul was going to far away cities like Damascus to hunt them down.
D. Biblical characters in the New Testament were never afraid to confess what they once had been. Paul told them of his past.

APPLICATION
A. God uses our past!
B. Philippians 3:13,14 - *...forgetting those things which are behind and reaching forward to those things which are ahead, I press toward the goal for the prize of the upward call of God in Christ Jesus.* (forget what obstructs you from the purpose of goal)
C. II Corinthians 1:1-6 - God uses our past to comfort and encourage others.

II. Paul Converted To Christ (V13-15)
A. Paul had a dramatic conversion. A light shined from heaven.
B. He was knocked to the ground and Jesus said, 'Saul, Saul, why are you persecuting Me?'
C. Jesus said, "It is hard for you to kick against the goads." Illustration: A goad is a sharp stick used to prod oxen, to a more rapid pace. Stephen's life and testimony must have have been a goad for Paul.
D. He said, "I am Jesus, whom you are persecuting. But rise and stand on your feet..."

APPLICATION:
A. Do you remember your conversion?
B. Your Damascus road experience?

III. Paul Called To Christ (V16-19)
A. He appeared to Paul for a purpose. The word to have appeared = op-tam-om-ahee = to gaze (ie. With eyes wide open to look at something remarkable. The word purpose = protue - es– is = is a setting forth a proposal or a purpose.
B. The purpose for this appearance was so Paul could become two things:
   1. A minister - hoop-ay-ref-ace - (to vow) an under-oarsman, an assistant, or a subordinate. Acting under another's directions.
      a. Paul has become a servant and assistant for Jesus in a way that he now acts on His behalf, making God's cause his own.
      b. He rowed according to directions.
      c. Called the carrier of shields or weapons because they have to always be ready to obey the one they are assisting.
   2. A witness - mar'-toos - a martyr, a record witness of the things he would be shown. We have been called to be ministers and witnesses.

C. He started as an apostle of the Sanhedran and ended as an apostle for Christ. God delivered him from the people and Gentiles and now was sending him as apostle. (a sent one!)

D. He was called to open the Gentile's eyes and turn them from darkness to light, from the power of Satan unto God. And God would give them forgiveness of sin and an inheritance (or lot) with the saints.

E. Paul was not disobedient to the heavenly vision. He was obedient to it. He did not just see the light, he walked in it. Paul did not just teach the gospel, but surrendered to the gospel. He was changed from Saul to Paul.

APPLICATION:
A. God has appeared to us for a purpose.
B. God wants to touch others through our lives.
C. The great value of the message is the changed lives it produces.

WILL YOUR ANCHOR HOLD IN THE STORMS OF LIFE?

Acts 27 - *And when it was decided that we should sail to Italy, they delivered Paul and some other prisoners to one named Julius, a centurion of the Augustan Regiment. 2 So, entering a ship of Adramyttium, we put to sea, meaning to sail along the coasts of Asia. Aristarchus, a Macedonian of Thessalonica, was with us. 3 And the next day we landed at Sidon. And Julius treated Paul kindly and gave him liberty to go to his friends and receive care. 4 When we had put to sea from there, we sailed under the shelter of Cyprus, because the winds were contrary. 5 And when we had sailed over the sea which is off Cilicia and Pamphylia, we came to Myra, a city of Lycia. 6 There the centurion found an Alexandrian ship sailing to Italy, and he put us on board. 7 When we had sailed slowly many days, and arrived with difficulty off Cnidus, the wind not permitting us to proceed, we sailed under the shelter of Crete off Salmone. 8 Passing it with difficulty, we came to a place called Fair Havens, near the city of Lasea. 9 Now when much time had been spent, and sailing was now dangerous because the Fast was already over, Paul advised them, 10 saying, "Men, I perceive that this voyage will end with disaster and much loss, not only of the cargo and ship, but also our lives." 11 Nevertheless the centurion was more persuaded by the helmsman and the owner of the ship than by the things spoken by Paul. 12 And because the harbor was not suitable to winter in, the majority advised to set sail from there also, if by any means they could reach Phoenix, a harbor of Crete opening toward the southwest and northwest, and winter there. 13 When the south wind blew softly, supposing that they had obtained their desire, putting out to sea, they sailed close by Crete. 14 But not long after, a tempestuous head wind arose, called Euroclydon. 15 So when the ship was caught, and could not head into the wind, we let her drive. 16 And running under the shelter of an island called Clauda, we secured the skiff with difficulty. 17 When they had taken it on board, they used cables to undergird the ship; and fearing lest they should run aground on the Syrtis Sands, they struck sail and so were driven. 18 And because we were exceedingly tempest-tossed, the next day they lightened the ship. 19 On the third day we threw the ship's tackle overboard with our own hands. 20 Now when neither sun nor stars appeared for many days, and no small tempest beat on us, all hope that we would be saved was finally given up. 21 But after long abstinence from food, then Paul stood in the midst of them and said, "Men, you should have listened to me, and not have sailed from Crete and incurred this disaster and loss. 22 And now I urge you to take heart, for there will be no loss of life among you, but only of the ship. 23 For there stood by me this night an angel of the God to whom I belong and whom I serve, 24 saying, 'Do not be afraid, Paul; you must be brought before Caesar; and indeed God has granted you all those who sail with you.' 25 Therefore take heart, men, for I believe God that it will be just as it was told me. 26 However, we must run aground on a certain island." 27 Now when the fourteenth night had come, as we were driven up and down in the Adriatic Sea, about midnight the sailors sensed that they were drawing near some land. 28 And they took soundings and found it to be twenty fathoms; and when they had gone a little farther, they took soundings again and found it to be fifteen fathoms. 29 Then, fearing lest we should run aground on the rocks, they dropped four anchors from the stern, and prayed for day to come. 30 And as the sailors were seeking to escape from the ship, when they had let down the skiff into the sea, under pretense of putting out anchors from the prow, 31 Paul said to the centurion and the soldiers, "Unless these men stay in the ship, you cannot be saved." 32 Then the soldiers cut away the ropes of the skiff and let it fall off. 33 And as day was about to dawn, Paul implored them all to take food, saying, "Today is the fourteenth day you have waited and continued without food, and eaten nothing. 34 Therefore I urge you to take nourishment, for this is for your survival, since not a hair will fall from the head of any of you." 35 And when he had said these things, he took bread and gave thanks to God in the presence of them all; and when he had broken it he began to eat. 36 Then they were all encouraged, and also took food themselves. 37 And in all we were two hundred and seventy-six persons on the ship. 38 So when they had eaten enough, they lightened the ship and threw out the wheat into the sea. 39 When it was day, they did not recognize the land; but they observed a bay with a beach, onto which they planned to run the ship if possible. 40 And they let go the anchors and left them in the sea, meanwhile loosing the rudder ropes; and they hoisted the mainsail to the wind and made for shore. 41 But striking a place where two seas met, they ran the ship aground; and the prow stuck fast and remained immovable, but the stern was being broken up by the violence of the waves. 42 And the soldiers' plan was to kill the prisoners, lest any of them should swim away and escape. 43 But the centurion, wanting to save Paul, kept them from their purpose, and commanded that those who could swim should jump overboard first and get to land, 44 and the rest, some on boards and some on parts of the ship. And so it was that they all escaped safely to land.*

INTRODUCTION
A. The Titanic, they boasted, was a ship that not even God could sink.
B. I Timothy 1:18-20 - *This charge I commit to you, son Timothy, according to the prophecies previously made concerning you, that by them you may wage the good warfare, having faith and good conscience, which some having rejected, concerning the faith have suffered shipwreck, of whom are Hymenaeus and Alexander, whom I delivered to Satan that they may learn not to blaspheme.*
C. Paul's voyage to Rome was filled with high adventure, danger, disasters and the intervention of the Lord.
D. Luke knew sailing terminology.
E. Let's look at our anchor and it's importance in the voyage of life with Jesus.

I. Voyage Will Be Stormy
A. They were determined to sail to Italy. Paul and the prisoners were delivered to Julius. Julius, a centurion, showed favor to Paul and gave him freedom to go to his friends.
B. Paul warned them the voyage would be different.
   1. You cannot have roses without thorns.
   2. Winds and waves will come in your life.
   3. Physical suffering. Will your anchor hold?
   4. The storm of death - Hebrews 9:27 - *And as it is appointed for men to die once, but after this the judgment...*
   5. Family problems will come.
   6. Financial problems will come.
   7. Emotional problems will come. Trust God. Matthew 14:22-33. "Peace be still."
C. The Christian life is full of challenges and victories. "Obstacles are all you see when you get your eyes off the goal." - Corky
D. We are called to be over comers. 1 John 5:4 - *For whatever is born of God overcomes the world. And this is the victory that has overcome the world - our faith.*

APPLICATION:
A. There will be storms on the voyage of the Christian life.
B. Keep your eyes on the goal.
C. Thank God for Christian friends.

II. The Vessel Must Be Seaworthy
A. When the wind came with force they started to go out of control. They had to use helps - the cables that held the ship together.
B. They threw things overboard that could cause the ship to sink. Is there anything we need to throw overboard in our ships?

1. Hebrews 12:1-2 - *Therefore we also, since we are surrounded by so great a cloud of witnesses, let us lay aside every weight, and the sin which so easily ensnares us, and let us run with durance the race that is set before us, looking unto Jesus, the author and finisher of our faith, who for the joy that was set before Him endured the cross, despising the shame, and has sat down at the right hand of the throne of God.*
       2. Look at Jesus and run with patience.
   C. Is any vessel seaworthy?
       1. Jesus.
       2. Noah pitched the ark with pitch. The vessel was sealed. Jesus has already gone through the storm. Jesus' blood has purchased safe passage.
   D. Paul declares there would be no loss of life. he angel of God told him he must come before Caesar and that God had given Paul all the men with him. He believed what God told him! Believe what God tells you.

APPLICATION:
   A. Believe God! He is with you.
   B. Get rid of anything that would cause you to sink.
   C. Get help!
   D. God makes us seaworthy in Him!

III. THE VALUABLES MUST BE SECURE!
   A. They were afraid when the fourteenth night had come. They were afraid they would run aground on the rocks. They wanted to abandon ship. Stay in the boat!
   B. They cast four anchors from the stern and prayed for day to come. What keeps the ship in your life off the rocks of despair and belief that God will use what you are going through?
       1. 1st anchor - The person of Christ - personal relationship (faith)
       2. 2nd anchor - The provision of Christ - all things added - seek first (surrender)
       3. 3rd anchor - The purpose of Christ - conform us to His image (hope)
       4. 4th anchor - The promise of Christ.
   C. Daylight will come!
   D. They gave thanks. They ate for their health. They were grounded, but all were alive and safe. Some swam, some were on boards and some were on broken pieces of the ship.

APPLICATION:
   A. He will not let us down.
   B. He will finish His work.
   C. Stay in the ship!
   D. There is no other safety.
   E. Get those anchors out in the night.

WHERE ARE THE MAKERS OF HISTORY?

Acts 28 - *Now when they had escaped, they then found out that the island was called Malta. 2 And the natives showed us unusual kindness; for they kindled a fire and made us all welcome, because of the rain that was falling and because of the cold. 3 But when Paul had gathered a bundle of sticks and laid them on the fire, a viper came out because of the heat, and fastened on his hand. 4 So when the natives saw the creature hanging from his hand, they said to one another, "No doubt this man is a murderer, whom, though he has escaped the sea, yet justice does not allow to live." 5 But he shook off the creature into the fire and suffered no harm. 6 However, they were expecting that he would swell up or suddenly fall down dead. But after they had looked for a long time and saw no harm come to him, they changed their minds and said that he was a god. 7 In that region there was an estate of the leading citizen of the island, whose name was Publius, who received us and entertained us courteously for three days. 8 And it happened that the father of Publius lay sick of a fever and dysentery. Paul went in to him and prayed, and he laid his hands on him and healed him. 9 So when this was done, the rest of those on the island who had diseases also came and were healed. 10 They also honored us in many ways; and when we departed, they provided such things as were necessary. 11 After three months we sailed in an Alexandrian ship whose figurehead was the Twin Brothers, which had wintered at the island. 12 And landing at Syracuse, we stayed three days. 13 From there we circled round and reached Rhegium. And after one day the south wind blew; and the next day we came to Puteoli, 14 where we found brethren, and were invited to stay with them seven days. And so we went toward Rome. 15 And from there, when the brethren heard about us, they came to meet us as far as Appii Forum and Three Inns. When Paul saw them, he thanked God and took courage. 16 Now when we came to Rome, the centurion delivered the prisoners to the captain of the guard; but Paul was permitted to dwell by himself with the soldier who guarded him. 17 And it came to pass after three days that Paul called the leaders of the Jews together. So when they had come together, he said to them: "Men and brethren, though I have done nothing against our people or the customs of our fathers, yet I was delivered as a prisoner from Jerusalem into the hands of the Romans, 18 who, when they had examined me, wanted to let me go, because there was no cause for putting me to death. 19 But when the Jews spoke against it, I was compelled to appeal to Caesar, not that I had anything of which to accuse my nation. 20 For this reason therefore I have called for you, to see you and speak with you, because for the hope of Israel I am bound with this chain." 21 Then they said to him, "We neither received letters from Judea concerning you, nor have any of the brethren who came reported or spoken any evil of you. 22 But we desire to hear from you what you think; for concerning this sect, we know that it is spoken against everywhere." 23 So when they had appointed him a day, many came to him at his lodging, to whom he explained and solemnly testified of the kingdom of God, persuading them concerning Jesus from both the Law of Moses and the Prophets, from morning till evening. 24 And some were persuaded by the things which were spoken, and some disbelieved. 25 So when they did not agree among themselves, they departed after Paul had said one word: "The Holy Spirit spoke rightly through Isaiah the prophet to our fathers, 26 saying, 'Go to this people and say: "Hearing you will hear, and shall not understand; And seeing you will see, and not perceive; 27 For the hearts of this people have grown dull. Their ears are hard of hearing, And their eyes they have closed, Lest they should see with their eyes and hear with their ears, Lest they should understand with their hearts and turn, So that I should heal them." ' 28 "Therefore let it be known to you that the salvation of God has been sent to the Gentiles, and they will hear it!" 29 And when he had said these words, the Jews departed and had a great dispute among themselves. 30 Then Paul dwelt two whole years in his own rented house, and received all who came to him, 31 preaching the kingdom of God and teaching the things which concern the Lord Jesus Christ with all confidence, no one forbidding him.*

INTRODUCTION

A. Tomorrow is the history that will be written.

B. What we often learn from history is we don't learn from history.

C. History repeats itself.

D. History is His story. The book of Acts is history on His story. This is the Acts of the Holy Spirit. Luke wrote about all that Jesus did and taught. He still wants to do and teach.

E. How do we fit into history? Will we be history makers? I know you say to yourself, "I have problems; I'm not significant anyway..." Don't let that stop you. Be a history maker! Three things characterize the makers of history.

I. A Spirit Of Compassion

A. The storms of life come and make us or shape us. The wind and waves come to change us. They were shipwrecked on Malta.

B. Paul showed compassion even by gathering a bundle of sticks. He served them.

C. The barbarians were unusually kind to the people.

D. The viper bit Paul and the barbarians immediately thought he was a murderer. It is important not to 'label' someone right away due to situations. Bad things happen to Christians.

E. Paul shook off the snake. We need to shake off the enemy and his grip. The barbarians changed their minds and thought Paul was a god. Be careful what people do to you when you minister to them. Point them to Jesus! We are what are by the grace of God.

F. Publius, the chief man of the island, had a father who was sick with a fever and dysentery. He and others were healed by God's power - the power of Jesus - supernatural power. Signs and wonders can draw people to Christ.

G. Do you have healing hands? History makers have compassionate hands & hearts.

APPLICATION:

A. The anointing of Isaiah 61:1-3 - *The Spirit of the Lord God is upon me, because the Lord has anointed me to preach good tidings to the poor; He has sent me to heal the brokenhearted, to proclaim liberty to the captives, and the opening of the prison to those who are bound; to proclaim the acceptable year of the Lord, and the day of vengeance of our God; to comfort all who mourn, to console those who mourn in Zion, to give them beauty for ashes, the oil of joy for mourning, the garment of praise for the spirit of heaviness; that they may be called trees of righteousness, the planting of the Lord, that He may be glorified.*

B. Minister to the sheep without a shepherd. Matthew 9:35-38 - *Then Jesus went about all the cities and villages, teaching in their synagogues, preaching the gospel of the kingdom, and healing every sickness and every disease among the people. But when He saw the multitudes, He was moved with compassion for them, because they were weary and scattered, like sheep having no shepherd. Then He said to His disciples, 'The harvest truly is plentiful, but the laborers are few. Therefore pray the Lord of the harvest to send out laborers into His harvest.'*

C. To whom and how can we show His compassion?

II. A Sense Of Community

A. As we minister to people we will be ministered to as well.

B. Ministry is not a one-way street. Paul thanked God and took courage. (v. 15)

C. The saints of God came to minister to Paul.

D. The Apostle Paul led a lonely life. We need each other.

APPLICATION:

A. We are the body of Christ.

B. Open your arms and heart to serve in the family.

C. Exodus 19:5-6 - *Now therefore, if you will indeed obey My voice and keep My covenant, then you shall be a special treasure to Me above all people; for all the earth is Mine. And you shall be to Me a kingdom of priests and a holy nation.' These are the words which you shall speak to the children of Israel."*

D. Reach out - give and receive.

III. A STRENGTH OF CONVICTION

A. The leaders of the Jews said they have heard of this sect.

B. We can compromise - we are tempted. NO COMPROMISE!

C. Will we listen to the voice of God and heed it and do it?

D. Paul proclaimed and testified about the Kingdom of God. Where ever Christ rules and reigns as King of kings and Lord of lords, there is the Kingdom of God. Some believed what Paul taught and some did not.

E. Paul prophesied out of Isaiah. They did not listen or see or understand. If they would have, God would have healed them. The salvation of God had been sent to the Gentiles.

F. Paul preached the Kingdom of God and taught things concerning the Lord Jesus Christ with all confidence! He preached and taught the kingdom in light of the King!

G. Receive all those that God brings to you.

APPLICATION:

A. Be a history maker!

B. Have a strength of conviction.

C. Preach and live Jesus - ask Him how He is building His Kingdom and how you can work with Him.

D. The storms and winds will not stop us...We will come to our Romes.

E. Let's start the 29th chapter of Acts with all of what Jesus began to do and teach through us.

BOOK OF ACTS
END NOTES

1   Morgan, G. Campbell. The Acts of the Apostles. Old Tappan, New Jersey: Fleming H. Revell Company, 1924.

2   Ogilvie, Lloyd John. The Communicators Commentary. Waco, TX: Word Books, 1983.

3   Barclay, William. The Acts of the Apostles. Louisville, Kentucky: Westminster Press, 1976.

4   Wagner, C. Peter. Acts of the Holy Spirit. Ventura, CA: Regal Books, 2000.

5   Ogilvie, Lloyd John. The Communicators Commentary. Waco, TX: Word Books, 1983.

6   Ogilvie, Lloyd John. The Communicators Commentary. Waco, TX: Word Books, 1983.

Made in the USA
Middletown, DE
17 September 2022

10654885R00057